THE RAILFAN GUIDE TO AUSTRIA

George H. Drury

© Copyright 1998 by George H. Drury. All rights reserved. This book may not be reproduced in part or in whole without written permission from the publisher, except in the case of brief quotations used in reviews. Published by George H. Drury, 4139 West McKinley Court, Milwaukee, WI 53208. Printed in U. S. A.

On the cover: Austrian Federal Railways local passenger trains meet at Obertraun, between Attnang-Puchheim and Stainach-Irdning, on April 26, 1989.

About the author: George Drury has been traveling by train on his own and as a group tour leader throughout North America and Europe since 1961. He has written rail travel articles for *Trains, Vintage Rails, International Railway Traveler,* and *Rail Travel Newsletter*. During his tenure as librarian of Kalmbach Publishing Co., publisher of *Trains* and *Model Railroader*, he compiled or edited most of the books in Kalmbach's Railroad Reference Series.

All photos are by the author except as noted in the captions.

ISBN 0-9665300-1-2

This book was prepared in May 1998, and reflects prices and schedules in effect then. Train times are from the March 1998 edition of the *Thomas Cook European Timetable* and the May 24, 1998–May 29, 1999, edition of *Fahrpläne*. Hotel prices and the star ratings are from the 1996/97 edition of *Hotels in Austria*, published by the Austrian National Tourist Office and the Austrian Hotel Association. Changes in prices, schedules, or conditions are inevitable. Hotel management can change, a waiter can have a bad day, and weather and crowds can alter the atmosphere of a place. If you find things greatly different from the way I've described them, please let me know. — GHD

Contents

Introduction 5
About Austria 9
    Geography 11
    Music 12
    Literature, architecture, and medicine 13
Language 14
    basic courtesies and necessities 14
    Railroad glossary 14
    Menu glossary 16
    Pronunciation 18
    Translations from the timetable 19
    Hotel reservation letters 20
Trip details
    Planning your trip 21
    Passes and tickets 23
    Before you go 26
    Now you're there 30
Austria's railways 35
    The lines 35
    Timetables 37
    Locomotives 38
    Passenger cars 41
    Riding the trains 42
Cities
    Amstetten 44
    Bischofshofen 50
    Bruck an der Mur 55
    Graz 60
    Innsbruck 65
    St. Pölten 72
    Salzburg 78
    Villach 86
    Wien 90
Odds and ends 100
Train times between major cities 103
Railway map of Austria 104
Index 106

KLAUS MATZKA'S VIEW of a double-headed container train ascending Semmering Pass in the golden sunshine of summer afternoon should provide sufficient justification for a railfan trip to Austria. But Austria has more than just high-density, electrified, double-track main lines over mountains — start turning pages to see what else there is.

INTRODUCTION

ON A MAP OF EUROPE most people can find England and France and Spain with no trouble. If you ask them to point out Austria, they'll be in trouble (a few will flip the pages of the atlas and confidently point to Sydney and Melbourne), and they'll confuse Vienna, the capital of Austria, with Venice, down in Italy.

Austria hasn't yet become a tourist destination to the extent that England, France, and Switzerland are. To begin with, Austria is well back in Europe. It's more than 600 miles from London to the west end of Austria. You have to fly over a lot of interesting, enticing places to get to Austria. Austria doesn't have a national symbol like Big Ben, the Eiffel Tower, or the Matterhorn. It doesn't have a national food like French wine or Swiss cheese and chocolate or German beer and sausages.

Okay, then, Austria is east of Switzerland, southeast of Germany, and northeast of Italy. Other countries that border on Austria are (starting at 12 and going clockwise) the Czech Republic, Slovakia, Hungary, and Slovenia — plus Liechtenstein, tucked between Switzerland and Austria west of Feldkirch. Austria has given the world Franz Josef Haydn, Wolfgang Amadeus Mozart, Johann Strauss and his waltzes, the Lippizaner horses, and *The Sound of Music*. Austria is more mountainous than Switzerland. It has railroads, too.

Why Austria?

The railfan will find variety: fast mainline railroading, mountain passes and tunnels, narrow gauge, steam, and streetcars. Austrian Federal Railways (ÖBB, Österreichische Bundesbahnen) offers more diversity of motive power than Switzerland, even if intriguing-looking antiques that were on the rails a few years ago have for the most part been replaced.

For the non-railfan, Austria offers a combination of mountain scenery and culture, the latter primarily in Vienna and Salzburg (although those cities have no monopoly on gilded baroque churches). The Austrian Empire put more time and energy into music and the arts than into defense and war, and some of that attitude is still around. Austria's people are open and friendly, and the food, beer, and wine are excellent.

Why Drury?

In 1980 I rode the Arlberg route to Innsbruck, explored the Zillertalbahn, and departed for Munich on the line through Garmisch-Partenkirchen. I was impressed with the prices in

Innsbruck — I'd just spent a night in Zürich. In 1985 I rode from Salzburg to Innsbruck, then back to Munich. The people in a model railroad shop in Innsbruck were pleasant, accepting deutsche mark traveler's checks with far less fuss than merchants in Germany. In 1988 I rode through Innsbruck on my way from Munich to Italy. By the time I got to Italy, I wished I'd stayed in Innsbruck.

In 1989 my interest was piqued by Rich and Caroline Tower's description of Austria: very much like Switzerland but less efficient. Karl-Dieter and Inge Bünting cited a hotel that was too close to the station in Villach — they recommended it for me but not for themselves. I spent ten days visiting Innsbruck, Bischofshofen, and St. Pölten. A description of that trip appeared in the June and July 1990 issues of *Trains*. In August of that year I led a Smithsonian tour to Vienna (hereinafter Wien), Graz, Villach, Badgastein, and Innsbruck.

In September 1991 I made a brief visit to Salzburg on a press trip showing the tourist attractions to a group of travel writers, but I escaped from the group to ride the Vöcklamarkt–Attersee Railway and the Salzburger Lokalbahn. A Smithsonian tour I led in June 1995 covered Wien, Salzburg, and Innsbruck. In October 1997 I spent a week going from Innsbruck to Wien via Lienz, Villach, Bruck an der Mur, and Amstetten — not the most direct route, but one that let me ride some narrow gauge lines. There are still parts of Austria I haven't explored, but I'll tell you what I know of the country and its railroads.

Notation

I use the German geographic names, because they are what you'll see and hear. Austria is Österreich, Vienna is Wien, and the Danube is the Donau. It's good to learn the local forms of place names. Let's say you're bound for Vienna. Your train rolls into Westbahnhof. You see signs reading "Wien." So do the people across the aisle, who say, "No, this is Wine, and they didn't even spell it right, and our travel agent said this train goes to Vienna, so we're going to stay put till we get there!"

Since you know that the people who live in Vienna call it Wien (pronounced Veen) you get off. Those folks across the aisle will soon find themselves in the coach yard.

I use metric units because that's what all my references are. More important, that's what's used there. The mile:kilometer ratio is 5:8, and the conversion factors are approximately 1.6 and 0.6. For purposes of answering "Is that too far to walk?" it's 2 miles for each 3 kilometers.

Train timetables use the 24-hour clock, so I do too. If you can't make the conversion easily, look through a discount store and you can probably find a digital watch with the 24-hour feature for less than $10.

The maps in the text will help you find the recommended hotels from the station, but don't try to scale distances off them.

In the schedule listings, a light underscore indicates a change of trains; a heavy underscore indicates the destination of the trip — the place to turn around and start back. After each departure time are timetable references for *Fahrpläne* (A) and the *Thomas Cook European Timetable* (C).

Innsbruck	leave	942	1342	(A3, C950)
Jenbach	arrive	1016	1516	
Jenbach	leave	1047	1452	(A31, C955)
Mayrhofen	arrive	1210	1610	
Mayrhofen	leave	1247	1647	

Occasionally I refer to circular trip itineraries as clockwise and counterclockwise. Imagine a clock face — a traditional clock, not a digital clock — on the map, or think of clockwise as making four right turns to go around the block.

One other timetable reference that you may encounter, most likely in German-language publications (but it's a handy and useful term) is KBS, for Kursbuchstrecke, which means timetable line. KBS 31 means the line shown in table 31 of the timetable (the national timetable, unless otherwise noted).

Schedules for recommended trips

I've quoted train times from the May 24, 1998–May 29, 1999, edition of *Fahrpläne,* the Austrian timetable book. If you're planning a complicated day with several connections, be sure to check current schedules.

I have started most of the suggested itineraries about 9:00 a.m. — 0900 — since you're on vacation. I have used Monday-to-Friday trains instead of weekend trains if there was a choice. Further, I have plotted minimum-time trips, with little time between trains to eat lunch or even catch your breath. Please take more time, if you wish. You're on vacation. Remember, too, that local trains give you a longer, more leisurely look at the scenery and the country than the expresses.

Acknowledgments

My first look at Austria was on a trip mapped out by J. H. Price, who was for many years editor of the *Thomas Cook European Timetable*. Since then I've had planning assistance from Rich and Caroline Tower and on-the-spot guidance from Chuck McDonald. Elisabeth Spiola and her staff at Mondial Travel in Wien mapped out that first Smithsonian tour, which was as educational for the tour leader as it was for the participants. Karl Zöchmeister and Klaus Matzka have kept me current on the rail situation in Austria. Joe Zucker helped me investigate the local lines around Salzburg. Ed Eisendrath, my travel agent, answered my questions even when he knew there was no ticket revenue involved. Bob Hayden offered much encouragement and assistance during the production of this guide. Marcia Stern rode herd on my spelling and grammar in early editions of this book. Mary Algozin proofread and edited this edition. I thank them all.

Then there's Maria Theresa (more formally Maria-Theresien Katze), acquired after that April 1989 trip, when I learned that nearly every Austrian city and town has something named for Empress Maria Theresa, so why not a cat? Her part in this project has been to lie across my reference materials or the pages I'm proofreading and walk across the com3333333333333333puter keyjjjjjjjjjjjjjjjjjjjboard.

George H. Drury

Milwaukee, Wisconsin
June 1998

ABOUT AUSTRIA

AUSTRIA WAS CONSOLIDATED in the 10th century as the eastern borderland of the Holy Roman Empire. From 1273 to 1806 Austria was ruled by the Habsburgs, who from time to time married into Spain, Italy, and the Netherlands; the dynasty also had a branch who were kings of France, and from 1864 to 1867 a Habsburg was emperor of Mexico.

Holy Roman Empire

The Holy Roman Empire (which has been characterized as neither holy nor Roman nor an empire) was a collection of Germanic and North Italian territories organized about 962, a vertical slice of Europe east of France, from Belgium and the Netherlands down to Rome. However, because of friction with the popes it became a trusteeship of the German states. In 1804, Francis II, emperor of the Holy Roman Empire, had himself proclaimed Francis I, Emperor of Austria. Napoleon insisted on abolition of the Holy Roman Empire, which was done in 1806.

As a result of the Congress of Vienna in 1814 and 1815, Austria lost Belgium and Breisgau (the region of Germany along the Rhine north of Basel), regained Salzburg and Galicia, and acquired Italian territory in Lombardy and Venetia. Austria became the leading power in Italy and assumed the presidency of the German confederation.

Post-1815 Austria comprised present-day Austria and Hungary plus Bohemia, Moravia, Galicia, Silesia, Slovakia, Transylvania, the Bukovina, Croatia-Slavonia, Carniola, Gorizia, Istria, Dalmatia, Lombardy, and Venetia. You'll have difficulty finding most of those on a modern map, but they constituted most of eastern Europe all the way down to Venice.

Austria included eleven nationalities and had no geographic or commercial unity. Various nationalities — Italians, Romanians, South Slavs — wanted to team up with others of the same nationality beyond the borders. Disintegration of Austria was inevitable.

Shrinkage

Emperor Ferdinand I reigned from 1835 to 1848, but he had an impaired mind, and the work of government was done by Archduke Louis, Prince Metternich, and Count Kolowrat — but Metternich and Kolowrat couldn't get along with each other, so little got done. In 1848 there were uprisings in France, Germany, and Italy. Metternich was ousted; a new constitution abolishing serfdom in Austria was adopted; and Ferdinand abdicated in favor of his 18-year-old nephew, Francis (or Franz) Joseph.

After war with Italy in 1859, Austria had to cede Lombardy and allow Italy to unify but it retained Venice. In 1866 Prussia allied with Italy; in a brief war that followed, Austria lost Venice and the dominance of Germany. In 1867 the Empire of Austria and the Kingdom of Hungary were united under a single monarch.

The period of shifting borders conincided with the construction of the railroads, accounting for some of the complexity of Austria's railroad map. The destination of a railway under construction had a good likelihood of suddenly being in some other country — or a stretch of railway itself could quickly wind up in foreign territory.

The Balkan Wars of 1912 stirred up matters east of Austria, with the Bulgarians, Serbs, Romanians, Greeks, and Turks all attacking each other. The major powers convened in London and managed to end those wars. The Treaty of Bucharest in 1913 established the size of European Turkey, created Albania, doubled the size of Serbia and Montenegro (however, without Albania, which they wanted), made Greece the most important power on the Aegean Sea, and left Bulgaria furious.

At that point Austria-Hungary consisted of (in present-day terms) those two countries plus the Czech Republic, Slovakia, much of what used to be Yugoslavia, southern Poland as far east as Lvov, and Italy from Brenner Pass south almost to Verona.

World War I

On June 28, 1914, Archduke Francis Ferdinand and his wife were assassinated at Sarajevo. Just one month later Austria declared war on Serbia. What should have been a local matter exploded into World War I.

Franz Josef died in 1916. Charles I took over and tried to patch things up, rather like Gerald Ford. He declared a federal state on October 16, 1918, and abdicated the thrones of Austria and Hungary on November 11 and 13, 1918.

In 1919 Austria was reduced to approximately one-fourth its former area and population. What remained was almost completely German-speaking, and the name of the country was chosen to reflect this: Deutsch-Österreich (German East State). At that time many Austrians wanted the country to join up with Germany. After a short period of dictatorship under Chancellor

Engelbert Dollfuss, Austria allied itself with Germany in 1938.

After World War II, Austria was occupied by Britain, France, Russia, and the United States. Full sovereignty was restored May 15, 1955. The country is neutral, but socially and economically it is part of the West.

GEOGRAPHY

Austria's position in Europe is that of a border or transition zone between Atlantic Europe and Danubian Europe — indeed, that was its earliest role back in the 900s. Extending from the west end of the country almost to Vienna, the Eastern Alps cover 71 percent of Austria's area (by contrast, 62 percent of Switzerland is mountainous).

Three major ranges form the Eastern Alps. The Northern Alps lie north of Innsbruck and south of Salzburg. The Inn, Salzach, and Enns rivers flow from west to east south of the Northern Alps, then turn north to flow through valleys into the Danube. The Central Alps lie south of those rivers. The Southern Alps run generally along the southern border of Austria.

North of the Alps is the valley of the River Danube (Donau in German), which flows eastward into the Hungarian Plain. North of the Danube lies forested hill country, the Bohemian Massif.

Austria's area is 34,306 square miles, bigger than Maine and smaller than Virginia. The population is about 7,500,000, about the same as Virginia plus the District of Columbia.

Lands

Austria is divided into nine provinces or lands. The map of Austria is shaped something like a tennis racket (really more like a pork chop, but a tennis racket is easier to discuss). Let's locate the nine provinces on the map (page 12). Farthest west, at the end of the handle, is Vorarlberg. It wanted to be part of Switzerland (it is, geographically), but Switzerland wouldn't have it. I don't know why. The capital is Bregenz, on Lake Konstanz.

Next, forming most of the handle of the racket, is Tirol; capital, Innsbruck. There's a separate piece, East Tirol, to the southeast. South Tirol was ceded to Italy in 1919 and is still largely German-speaking. The Tiroleans were the emperor's chosen people, sort of — they were allowed to address him with the familiar "du" instead of the formal "Sie."

Where the handle joins the body of the racket is the province of Salzburg; its capital is the city of Salzburg. Along the upper side of the body are Upper Austria and Lower Austria, Ober-

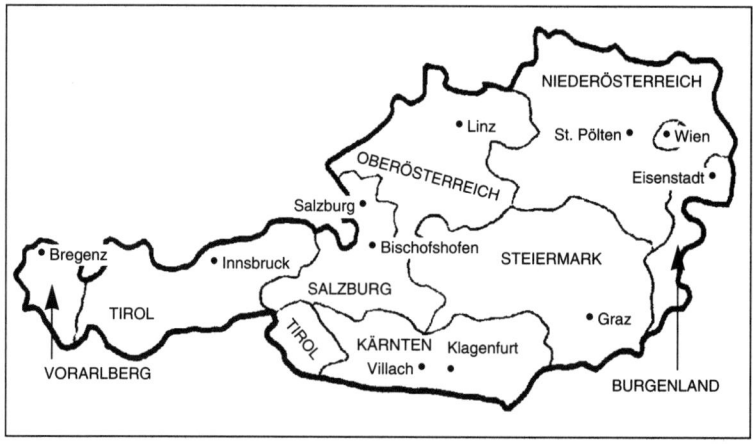

österreich and Niederösterreich. The capital of Upper Austria is Linz. The capital of Lower Austria is the city of St. Pölten, 60 kilometers west of Wien. Lower Austria surrounds the city of Vienna (Wien), which is itself a province.

Along the lower side of the body is Carinthia — Kärnten in German. Its capital is Klagenfurt. It is drained by the River Drau, which flows southeast into what was Yugoslavia. It has a milder climate than the rest of Austria. Filling in the rest of the body of the racket is Styria, or Steiermark. Its capital is Graz. The rim of the racket farthest from the handle is Burgenland, which was acquired from Hungary after World War I. Its capital is Eisenstadt.

The largest province is Lower Austria, with 7,402 square miles. The smallest and the most populous is Vienna — 1.5 million inhabitants, about a fifth of the country's population.

About one-third of Austria is covered with forest. Natural resources include salt, iron, lignite, oil, and gas. Industry, which is heavily nationalized, includes iron, steel, and aluminum plus the fuel industries.

MUSIC

The Golden Age of Viennese culture was around 1850. For all the difficulty the Austria emperors had with foreign and domestic affairs, they were successful at encouraging the arts, notably music. Most classical music, the music you find on the program of the big symphony orchestras, is the product of composers who at the very least spent some time in Vienna. Austria's composers include Franz Josef Haydn (1732-1809), Wolfgang Amadeus Mozart (1756-1791), Ludwig van Beethoven

(1770-1827), Johannes Brahms (1833-1897), Johann Strauss the younger (1825-1899), Franz Lehar (1870-1948), Anton Bruckner (1824-1896), and Gustav Mahler (1860-1911). I mention these composers because some of them have trains named for them.

LITERATURE, ARCHITECTURE, MEDICINE

We are handicapped in knowing Austrian literature by the language barrier — music does not have that problem. Among the literary names you may encounter are those of dramatist Franz Grillparzer (1791-1872), novelist Adalbert Stifter (1805-1868), and dramatist Johann Nestroy (1801-1862). More recent names include poet Rainer Marie Rilke (1875-1926), Franz Kafka (1883-1924), and Stefan Zweig (1881-1942).

Architectural styles you have heard of and will encounter, especially in Wien, include Baroque, Biedermeier, and Jugenstil (Art Nouveau). A name you probably haven't heard is that of Friedensreich Hundertwasser. It is worth a trip to the corner of Löwengasse and Kegelgasse in Wien to see the apartment house he designed — curves, bright colors, even lumpy pavement. Take the U3 subway line to Rochusgasse, one stop east of Wien Mitte and walk a little way northeast, or take streetcar line N and get off at Hetzgasse or Löwengasse.

In science and medicine one name stands out above all the others, that of Sigmund Freud. He has probably had a greater influence on modern-day casual conversation than any other Austrian — or European.

Before you go, skim through the background chapters of whichever general tourist guidebook you've chosen. It will give you an acquaintance with the names and concepts — not a deep enough acquaintance that you could write a term paper or a master's thesis, but enough so that next time you hear the name or the concept, you'll feel a warm glow of recognition (you might even pick up enough knowledge for bluffing purposes, but that's not the purpose of this guidebook).

LANGUAGE

THE LANGUAGE OF AUSTRIA is German. Many Austrians speak and understand English, but knowledge of German will enrich your experience. Consider signing up for an evening course in conversational German at your local community college.

There are lots of language instruction books. My brother recommends *Just Enough German*. Phrase books contain a lot of material you don't need. For example, don't bother learning the words for bandage, splint, tourniquet, and ambulance. If you need those, it will be obvious.

A college friend once said the only German you need is "Ja," "Nein," "Ein Bier, bitte," "Noch ein Bier, bitte," and "Hilfe! Rette mich!" (yes; no; a beer, please; another beer, please; and help! save me!). I'd add "Wo ist die Toilette?"

Peg Bracken says the most useful foreign-language phrases are the equivalents of "Does anyone here speak English?" "Not right now, please," and "Go away." ("Spricht jemand hier Englisch?" "Nicht in diesem Moment, bitte," and "Geh weg.")

Here are several glossaries: basic necessities, railroad terms, and menu words, the last arranged German to English, since that's how you'll encounter them.

Two words you'll encounter in old railway names are "königliche" and "kaiserliche," which mean "royal" and "imperial" respectively. The funny-looking letter "ß" is pronounced like "ss" (it's called "ess-zet," ess zee).

BASIC COURTESIES AND NECESSITIES

Do you speak English?	Sprechen Sie Englisch?
Please	Bitte
Thank you	Danke, danke schön
You're welcome	Bitte schön
Hello	Grüß Gott
Good morning, good day	Guten Morgen, Guten Tag
Good evening, good night	Guten Abend, Gute Nacht
Toilet	der Abort, die Toilette
Ladies' room	die Damentoilette
Men's room	die Herrentoilette

RAILROAD GLOSSARY

Arrival	die Ankunft
Baggage	das Gepäck
Baggage car	der Gepäckwagen

Car (railroad)	der Wagen
Customs	der Zoll
Departure	die Abfahrt
Diesel locomotive	die Diesellok
Dining car	der Speisewagen
Direction (toward)	die Richtung
Electric locomotive	die Ellok
Express train	der Schnellzug
First class	erste Klasse
Forbidden	verboten
Late	verspätet
Local train	der Regionalzug
Locomotive	die Lok, Lokomotive
Main station	der Hauptbahnhof (Hbf)
Narrow gauge railway	die Schmalspurbahn
Nonsmoking car	der Nichtraucher
Operation	der Betrieb
Passenger car	der Reisezugwagen
Platform (station)	der Bahnsteig, der Perron
Rack or cog railway	die Zahnradbahn
Railcar (powered)	der Triebwagen
Railbus	der Schienenbus
Railfan	der Eisenbahnfreund
Railway	die Eisenbahn, die Bahn
Reserved	reserviert
Reservations	die Platzreservierung
Seat	der Platz
Second class	zweite Klasse
Service, traffic	der Verkehr
Shops	die Werkstätte
Sleeping car	der Schlafwagen
Smoking car	der Raucher
Station	der Bahnhof (Bhf)
Steam locomotive	die Dampflok
Stop	der Aufenthalt
Street	die Straße
Ticket	die Fahrkarte
Track	das Gleis
Track gauge	die Spurweite
Train	der Zug
Train from	der Zug von
Train to	der Zug nach
Yard	der Verschiebebahnhof (Vbf)

Language 15

MENU GLOSSARY

I've included the definite articles so that if you're offered something you don't want, you can decline it correctly. I have given the plural form for things you are unlikely to encounter singly, such as beans and raspberries. Some terms are unique to Austria, such as "Erdapfel" for potato. This list also includes the German terms.

die Ananas	Pineapple
die Ananas(erdbeeren) (Aust.)	Large strawberries
der Apfel	Apple
die Aprikose	Apricot
das Bier (vom Faß)	Beer (from the tap)
der Blumenkohl	Cauliflower
das Brot, -brot	Bread, sandwich
der Champignon	Mushroom
das Ei, die Eier	Egg, eggs
das Eis	Ice cream
der Erdapfel (Aust.)	Potato
die Erdbeeren	Strawberries
das Faschiertes (Aust.)	Minced meat
die Fisolen (Aust.)	Green beans
das Fleisch	Meat
die Gabel	Fork
das Gemüse	Vegetable
das Glas	Glass
die grünen Bohnen	Green beans
die Himbeeren	Raspberries
die Jagdspezialitäten	Hunt specialties (game)
der Kaffee	Coffee
das Kalbfleisch	Veal
der Karfiol (Aust.)	Cauliflower
die Karotte	Carrots
die Kartoffeln	Potatoes
der Käse, das Käsebrot	Cheese, cheese sandwich
der Kohl	Cabbage
das Kotelett	Cutlet
der Kren (Aust.)	Horseradish
die Leber	Liver
der Löffel	Spoon
die Marille (Aust.)	Apricot
die Melange (Aust.)	Coffee with milk
die Melanzana (Aust.)	Eggplant
das Messer	Knife

die Milch	Milk
der Nachtisch	Dessert
die Niere	Kidneys
die Nudeln	Noodles
das Obers (Aust.)	Whipped cream
das Obst	Fruit
der Paradiesapfel, Paradieser, Paradeiser (Aust.)	Tomato
der Pfeffer	Pepper
das Reh	Venison
das Rind, das Rindfleisch	Beef
die Rippe, die Rippen	Rib, ribs
der Rosenkohl	Brussels sprouts
der Saft	Juice
die Sahne	Cream
das Salz	Salt
der Schinken	Ham
das Schlagobers (Aust.)	Whipped cream
der Schnitt	Slice; open-face sandwich
das Schwein	Pork
die Semmel (Aust.)	Roll
die Serviette	Napkin
der Speck	Bacon
die Speisekarte	Menu
der Spieß	Skewer, spit, or something on one
die Steinpilze	Mushrooms
die Stelze (Aust.)	Leg of pork
das Tagesmenu	Daily special meal
der Tagesteller	Daily plate special
die Tasse	Cup
der Tee	Tea
die Teigwaren	Pasta
der Teller	Plate
der Toast	Grilled-cheese sandwich
der verlängerter Kaffee	Diluted or stretched coffee
die Vorspeise	Appetizer
das Wasser	Water
der Wein (offener Wein)	Wine (open wine – available by the glass)
Rot, weiß	Red, white
die Wurst, die Würste	Sausage, sausages
der Zucker	Sugar
die Zwiebeln	Onions

PRONUNCIATION

The following list is no substitute for a course in conversational German, but it should give you something to work from.

Consonants

German	English equivalent
b	same
ch	ch as in loch, if you're a Scot; about the same sound as you get from an angry cat
d	same
f	same
g	g as in good or get
h	same, except in such words as gehen and sehen, where the h serves to lengthen the first e but is otherwise silent
j	y, as in yard or yet
k	same
l	l as in long or lily
m	same
n	same
p	same
qu	kv
r	pronounced with a single flip of the tongue
s	ss as in class, except like the s in rose at the beginning of a word or before "en"
ß	ss, as in class
sch	sh
t	same
th	t
tsch	ch as in chimney
v	f as in frank
w	v as in vase
z	ts, as in hats

Vowels

German	English equivalent
a	a as in father
ä, ae	ai as in claim
ai	i as in high
au	ow as in owl
äu, aeu	oy
e	eh; before a double consonant or two consonants it becomes the e sound in egg
ei	i as in high
eu	oy
i	i as in bit
ie	ee as in feet
o	o as in open; before a double consonant or two consonants it becomes the o sound in clock
ö, oe	the vowel sound of girdle, with no r sound in it
u	u as in nude
ü, ue	put your lips into position for an oo, then say ee

A doubled vowel or a vowel followed by h is pronounced the same but held longer. Two consonants or a double consonant after a vowel shorten the vowel sound.

TRANSLATIONS FROM THE TIMETABLE

Fahrpläne is entirely in German. A few words and phrases that occur in footnotes are worth listing. Most of the symbols are easy to decode. The codes for days of operation are the most likely to trip you up. A circled A means Monday through Friday; a circled B, daily except Saturday; and a circled C means Saturday, Sunday, and holidays. Dates in footnotes are of the form 6.VIII, which means August 6 (6th day, VIIIth month).

Abteil	compartment, section
an, am	on, on the
Ankunft	arrival
Anschluß	connection
außer	except
bis	to, as far as
Eilzug	reasonably fast train
Fahrplanbild	table
Feiertage	holidays
halt nur nach Bedarf	stops only on request
jedoch	however
keine Anschluß	no connection
Kurswagen	through car
mindestens	at least
nach	to
nicht	not
ohne	except
Schnellzug	fast train
Seite	page
sowie	also
täglich	daily
Übergangszeit	connection time
umsteigen	change trains
verkehrt (nicht)	operates (not)
von, vom	from, from the
weitere Züge	additional trains
Werktagen	work days
Zug führt nur ...	train carries only ...
Zugverbindungen	connections

HOTEL RESERVATION LETTERS

You can be reasonably sure a letter in English will be understood, but it's polite to write it in German. I do it twice, first in German to be polite, then in English to be sure I'm asking for what I think I'm asking for. To avoid possible confusion, spell out the month instead of using numbers and slashes. Europeans express dates as day/month/year.

You will find it considerably faster to fax your reservation request. My experience is that faxed reservation requests get an immediate answer, particularly if I get up in the small hours to send them at cheap rates. About the time I go back to sleep the phone rings and I hear the noise of the fax machine.

English equivalent

Dear Sirs,

I plan to travel in Austria and would like to make a reservation in your hotel for 1 room/2 rooms for 1 person/2 persons, arriving on (date) and leaving on (date).

Please confirm if a room is available and the cost for a room with/without bath/shower and toilet.

Sincerely,

German

Sehr geehrte Herren,

Ich beabsichtige, eine Reise in Österreich zu unternehmen und mich in Ihrem Hotel aufzuhalten. Darf ich Sie daher bitten, 1 Zimmer/2 Zimmer für 1 Person/2 Personen vom (arrival date) bis (departure date) auf meinen Namen zu reservieren.

Ich wäre Ihnen dankbar, wenn Sie mir mitteilen könnten, ob für die gewünschten Daten noch Unterkunft verfügbar ist und was die Kosten für ein Zimmer mit/ohne Bad/Dusche und WC betragen.

Mit freundlichen Grüßen,

Hotel term glossary

hotel	Hotel
I would like	ich möchte
double room, single room	Doppelzimmer/Einzelzimmer
with, without	mit, ohne
shower, bath, toilet	Dusche, Bad, Toilette

TRIP DETAILS

PLANNING YOUR TRIP

Travel agents

Travel agents understand airline fares and schedules and have direct access to airline computers without having to hear "All our agents are busy helping other customers with their travel plans. Your call will be answered in the order in which it was received" (Translation: We don't have enough people on the payroll). Traditionally travel agents have made their money from commissions paid by airlines and hotels and have usually made no charge for their services. The airlines recently cut commissions, and many travel agents now charge a fee. The expertise and the convenience is probably worth the fee for your air ticket. You may be better off making the hotel reservations yourself by letter or fax.

Where to start and where to finish

Austrian Airlines and Delta fly between New York (JFK) and Wien. You may find it more convenient (or more rewarding in the matter of frequent flier miles) to fly to Frankfurt, Munich, or Zürich, then take a connecting flight to Wien, Graz, Innsbruck, Salzburg, Linz, or Klagenfurt. Or at that point you may have had enough flying and be ready for a train ride.

Munich is a good gateway for Salzburg and Innsbruck. There is frequent train service between the Munich airport and the Munich Hauptbahnhof, the main station. From there trains run every hour or so to Salzburg (running time 1:30 to 2:00) and Innsbruck (1:35 to 3:20, depending on the route).

Zürich is a good gateway for points west of Innsbruck. Five trains per hour make the 11-minute trip from Zürich airport to Zürich Hauptbahnhof. Trains leave there at 0933 and 1333 for Innsbruck. Zürich to Bludenz is about 2 hours; Zürich to Innsbruck is about 4 hours. Trains leave Zürich airport at 0745, 0945, 1345, and 1745 and reach Bregenz at 0921, 1121, 1521, and 1921.

A nonstop flight from your home city right to your destination is best, but most people will have to change planes at least once. If you have a choice, and if other factors such as fare and departure and arrival times are equal, plan your itinerary so that the connections occur early in your trip in both directions. Denver-Chicago-Frankfurt, for example, is easier than Denver-Boston-Frankfurt, because you are fresher when you make the change. Frankfurt-Boston-Denver is better than Frankfurt-Chicago-Denver, because you get a chance to stretch your legs about an hour sooner. Try to avoid New York, especially if your itinerary requires a transfer between JFK and La Guardia — and if it does, allow at least 3 hours for the transfer, and remember that you can't check baggage through.

Solo versus group travel

Some people can travel alone; others can't. I think it depends on whether you live alone and whether you speak and understand the local language. Hotels, like Noah, expect their guests to come in pairs and price their rooms accordingly.

Group travel can also have drawbacks. If you are just two people with different interests, at least one of you will have to compromise. A group of four — two couples, let's say — can split up at least two ways. The men can go track down another streetcar line or narrow gauge railway while the women find an art gallery; the two couples can go their own ways.

My sole small-group experience was with eight persons, three couples and two singles, four rail enthusiasts and four not. We divided into almost all possible combinations for train-riding, sightseeing, shopping, and so on. It worked fine. More than eight and you'll have difficulty getting everyone around the same dinner table, and that is one of the benefits of group travel — you have someone to talk with at dinner.

Group tours

I'm certainly not opposed to group tours, since I lead them, but study the itinerary carefully before you sign up. A tour that moves by bus (and the proper travel industry word for bus is "coach" or sometimes even "luxury motor coach") to visit ten places where you can see and buy traditional Austrian embroidery in eight days won't give you much chance to see and ride trains.

There are group tours that specialize in railroads — you'll see them advertised in *International Railway Traveler* and *Trains*. A general-purpose tour that moves by train and offers occasional free time ("afternoon at leisure") may be a compromise that ensures domestic peace. Your tour leader might be a railfan who can suggest things to do on those free afternoons.

When to go

Go when you can get the vacation time. My preferences are May and September, before and after the main tourist season.

September is likely to be warmer than May; May offers longer days. Toward the end of September the weather can turn cool, and my experience on several trips is that the middle of October marks the end of good traveling weather.

Watch out for holidays. Austria celebrates lots of them.

	1999	2000	2001	2002	2003
New Year's Day	Jan. 1	Jan. 1	Jan. 1	Jan. 1	Jan. 1
Epiphany	Jan. 6	Jan. 6	Jan. 6	Jan. 6	Jan. 6
Good Friday	April 2	April 21	April 13	March 29	April 18
Easter	April 4	April 23	April 15	March 31	April 20
Easter Monday	April 5	April 24	April 16	April 1	April 21
Labor Day	May 1	May 1	May 1	May 1	May 1
Ascension Day	May 13	June 1	May 24	May 9	May 29
Pentecost Monday	May 24	June 12	June 4	May 20	June 9
Corpus Christi	June 3	June 22	June 13	May 30	June 19
Feast of Assumption	Aug. 15	Aug. 15	Aug. 15	Aug. 15	Aug. 15
Flag Day	Oct. 26	Oct. 26	Oct. 26	Oct. 26	Oct. 26
All Saints Day	Nov. 1	Nov. 1	Nov. 1	Nov. 1	Nov. 1
Immac. Conception	Dec. 8	Dec. 8	Dec. 8	Dec. 8	Dec. 8
Christmas	Dec. 25	Dec. 25	Dec. 25	Dec. 25	Dec. 25
St. Stephen's Day	Dec. 26	Dec. 26	Dec. 26	Dec. 26	Dec. 26

Austrian National Tourist Offices

• 500 North Michigan Avenue, Suite 1950, Chicago, IL 60611. Phone 312-644-8029.

• 1300 Post Oak Boulevard, Suite 960, Houston, TX 77056. Phone 713-850-9999.

• 11601 Wilshire Boulevard, No. 2480, Los Angeles, CA 90025. Phone 310-477-3332.

• 1010 Ouest Rue Sherbrook, No. 1410, Montreal, PQ H3A 2R7. Phone 514-849-3709.

• 500 Fifth Avenue, No. 2009, New York, NY 10110. Phone 212-944-6880.

• 2 Bloor Street East, No. 3330, Toronto, ON M4W 1A8. Phone 416-967-3381.

• 736 Granville Street, No. 1220, Vancouver, BC V6Z 1J2. Phone 604-683-8695.

Tourist guidebooks

There are lots of guidebooks. Fodor is heavier on hotels and restaurants; Baedeker is good for sightseeing. I've just bought a copy of the Lonely Planet guide to Austria, and I think it's better than the first two.

One-night stands

Packing up and moving every day is tiring. Plan to spend at least two nights at most of your stops. Austria is compact enough that you can easily move from one stop to the next and still have time that day for activities beyond just getting from one place to the next.

PASSES AND TICKETS

If you plan to cross national borders by train, the Eurailpass is your best buy. It offers unlimited first-class train travel and covers fast-train supplementary fares (seat reservations are 30 schillings extra).

Passes are valid for six months after they are issued; you validate the passes by presenting them at a ticket window before your first train ride. The Eurail Saverpass is available for two persons traveling together. 1998 U. S. dollar prices for the Eurailpass and Eurail Saverpass are:

	Single person (Eurailpass)	Each of two persons (Eurail Saverpass)
15 consecutive days of travel	$538	$458
21 days	$698	$594
1 month	$864	$734
2 months	$1224	$1040
3 months	$1512	$1286

Children under 12 are half fare; under 4 free.

Eurail Flexipass

The Eurailpass is for consecutive days, a solid block of time. On a day when you don't ride a train at all, the meter on the pass keeps ticking. If you're planning a trip where you will alternate days of train riding with days of in-depth city exploration, you may want to consider the Eurail Flexipass. It is valid for a certain number of days of travel within a two-month period. Prices are:

	Single person	Each of two persons
10 days of travel in 2 months	$634	$540
15 days of travel in 2 months	$836	$710

EuroPass

The EuroPass is good for five days of first-class travel in the five most popular countries: France, Germany, Italy, Spain, and Switzerland. As with the Eurailpass, there is a discount for two persons traveling together.

	Single person	Each of two persons
5 days of travel in 2 months	$326	$261
with 1 associate country	$386	$309
with 2 associate countries	$416	$333
with 3 associate countries	$436	$349
with all 4 associate countries	$446	$357
additional days (up to 10), each	$42	$33.50

The associate countries are BeNeLux (Belgium, Netherlands, and Luxembourg); Austria and Hungary; Portugal; and Greece (including the ferry from Italy).

Eurail Youthpass

The Eurail Youthpass is available for persons under 26. It's good for second-class travel and it covers fast-train surcharges.

	Single person
15 days	$376
21 days	$489
1 month	$605
2 months	$857
3 months	$1059
10 days of travel in 2 months	$444
15 days of travel in 2 months	$555

A second-class youth version of the EuroPass costs $216 for 5 days; additional days are $29, and the additional countries are correspondingly less.

European East Pass

The European East Pass is valid for rail travel in Austria, Hungary, Czech Republic, Slovakia, and Poland.

	First class
5 days of travel in 15 days	$199
Extra days (up to 5)	$22

Austrian Railpass

The Austrian Railpass is valid on ÖBB and yields discounts on cog railways and boats.

	First class	Second class
3 days in 15	$145	$98
Additional days (up to 5), each	$21	$15

Stern & Hafferl offers a pass (Umweltkarte) good on all its operations. Two persons can share the card.

Many transit systems offer a 24-hour pass. Vienna offers 24- and 72-hour tickets that are valid on all the public transportation services in the tariff area. You can purchase them from machines in the subway stations.

How to get passes

You must purchase your Eurailpasses before leaving North America, and you'll feel more secure buying the other passes here rather than in Europe — in a foreign currency and a foreign language. Your travel agent can get the passes for you, or you can buy them from Rail Europe (800-4-EURAIL, then press 2) or DER Travel Services (800-717-4247).

Timetables

The Austrian timetable, *Fahrpläne,* is not available in North America. The *Thomas Cook European Timetable* is good for starters. You can get it from Forsyth Travel Library, (phone 800-FORSYTH — or 800-367-7984). Price is $27.95 plus $4.95 for shipping (the shipping charge is good for up to three items). Forsyth accepts MasterCard and VISA. Cook's web site is http://thomascook.co.uk

You can buy a copy of *Fahrpläne* at any station in Austria. The price is 115 schillings. The price includes a 64-page supplement showing the long-distance trains.

In the itineraries for the suggested trips I have cited the table numbers in *Fahrpläne* and the *Thomas Cook European Timetable,* coding the table numbers A and C.

Maps

The *Thomas Cook Rail Map of Europe* shows you which lines are electrified, which are narrow gauge, and so on. You can order it along with the timetable.

Readers of previous editions of this guide recommend the *Eisenbahn und Schiffahrtskarte der Republik Oesterreich*, a 1:500,000 map published in 1985 by UK Quail Map Co. and available from Arnold Joseph, Room 701, 1140 Broadway, New York, NY 10001; and the Freytag & Berndt *Oesterreich Touring Atlas,* a road atlas that shows rail lines (ISBN 3-85084-021-2).

If you have a good map store nearby or a bookstore with a good travel section, see what you can find there.

BEFORE YOU GO

Documents

You'll need a passport. How do you get one? Ask your travel agent, check U.S. Government listings in the phone book, or ask at the post office.

If your cameras are foreign-made, it's possible to register them with U.S. customs before you leave so you won't have to pay duty on them when you return. If you live in a place without a customs office, I imagine you could do this at the airport before you leave. However, I've carried those registration certificates for years, and no one has ever asked to see them.

The customs office or your travel agent can give you a leaflet about how much of what you can bring back with you.

Money

The unit of currency is the schilling, abbreviated "S" in Austria; internationally "ÖS" or "ATS." In late June 1998 the schilling ran about 12.7 to the dollar or 7.9 cents each. The schilling is divided into 100 groschen, but it's unlikely you'll encounter any. A bank gave me a 2-groschen and a 5-groschen coin. If a bank gives something away, it can't be worth much.

U. S. dollar travelers checks are still the easiest way to carry money. Banks and the exchange counters in railway stations and airports offer the official rate of exchange, a better rate than you'll get at a hotel desk. However, sometimes the convenience of the hotel desk is worth the extra cost — a rainy Sunday evening, for example. One bank may offer a better rate than another, but searching for optimum exchange rates isn't the reason you came to Austria. Sometimes the rate includes the commission or fee for the transaction; sometimes it doesn't. If the fee is per transaction, cash two or three checks at a time.

Visa, MasterCard, and American Express cards are widely accepted in Austria, but don't count on months of float. Every time I've used a credit card in Europe the transaction has appeared on the next month's statement.

Luggage

The basic rule is "Two pieces max." You have two hands max. The combination that works best for me is a small over-the-shoulder bag for things like camera and sunglasses (for ten years I've used a Lands' End Lighthouse Attaché) and a large suitcase with wheels and a towing strap for the once-a-day items. Other people I've traveled with echo approval of luggage with wheels.

There are two types of wheeled suitcases. Those with four wheels have all their weight on the wheels and none on your arm, but the wheels are vulnerable, expecially the ball-bearing casters at the front. The other type has two wheels at the rear and a handle at the front. You carry about half the weight, but the suitcase is easier to control (four-wheelers flop over on their sides if you take a corner too fast) and the wheels are less vulnerable to mistreatment between the airline check-in counter and the baggage-claim carousel.

Another consideration is size. I traveled for several years with a 28-inch Pullman (the name was originally applied to a suitcase designed to fit under a Pullman section seat). I found it too large to fit on baggage racks in passenger cars, and large enough that fully loaded it weighed 50 to 60 pounds. I haven't used a collapsible luggage cart, but it's another item to have on your mind and it requires setup and take-down.

Don't overlook the convenience of checking baggage through if you're going from A to C with a stop of several hours at B. The charge for checking baggage is 90 schillings per piece within Austria and 140 schillings internationally. Weight limits are 50 kilograms within Austria and 25 kilograms (55 pounds) internationally. Not all trains carry checked baggage, so your baggage may not arrive at the same time you do — check the timetable notes.

At many stations you can check your baggage for several hours or the day for 30 schillings.

Clothing

My feeling is that you're more likely to get through Immigration and Customs if you don't look as if you will drag down the average. To put it another way, don't dress like you would to grot out the pigsty, and I know some American railfans who do.

You might want to have a coat and tie available (or skirt, depending on your gender) if you plan to dine in a top-bracket restaurant. Other than that, men won't need anything more formal than a blazer or sport coat over an open-collar shirt, with chinos or jeans below. Women can wear slacks or jeans.

Men's clothing

I take:
- A tweed sport coat or a lightweight blazer, mostly to wear over the sportshirt du jour at dinnertime.
- Water-repellent jacket and hat — easier to stow in the shoulder

bag than a full-length raincoat. Unlike an umbrella, a hat leaves your hands free.
• A light folding plastic or nylon raincoat for protection against the occasional deluge.
• A sweater.
• Two or three pairs of slacks.
• One change of underwear and socks per day.
• One shirt per day-and-a-half.
• Bathrobe, slippers, pajamas — bathrobe only if I'm staying in hotels where the bathroom is down the hall; pajamas are your choice. Some travel books suggest that a bathrobe can add warmth to pajamas (or whatever) if you get cold during the night. I try this about once every ten years and wake up with the bathrobe hopelessly twisted around me.
• Two pairs of comfortable, supportive, sturdy shoes. For a long time I advocated only sturdy leather soles. Then I bought a pair of Rockport Dressports with foam-Vibram soles — they and several successor pairs have been my traveling shoes ever since.

Women's clothing

My sister-in-law's advice is to wear something on the plane you won't need to wear again until you have a chance to wash it. Many travel books suggest a wardrobe plan — one or two colors and everything going with everything else. This isn't bad advice for guys either, if such things matter to you.

Laundry

Some travel authorities wash clothes every night, hang them up over the tub, and hope they're dry in the morning. Others suggest you buy cheap clothing for the trip, wear it once, and throw it away. No — buy your usual underwear and socks and leave them home. Take your tired, worn-out things and discard them day by day.

If I am going for two weeks or less, I pack for the whole trip. Doing laundry isn't much fun even at home. Plastic bags can separate the dirty from the clean in the suitcase.

The hotel desk can sometimes steer you in the direction of a laundromat (Münzwäscherei). The one in Innsbruck I used in 1980 was gone when I checked in 1997. Hotels often offer one- or two-day laundry service. It is usually extremely expensive.

You can get it there

As you head to the airport and do a mental inventory of the suitcase, remember that you can buy almost anything you've forgotten. The exception is spare parts. Take a second pair of glasses, for example, or whatever the breakage or loss of will inconvenience or discomfort you.

Home front

Most travel books are full of checklists of things to do before you leave: stop the newspaper, give the key to a neighbor, put a couple of lamps on timers. Something they don't tell you to do is to have food in the cupboard or the freezer that you can prepare with a minimum of effort when you get home.

Uncommon colds

My theory is that you have a resistance to local germs, but the cold germs elsewhere are different. Combine that with the dry air on the plane, changes of altitude, and fatigue, and it is likely, I'm sorry to say, you will catch a cold. Carry along a package of whatever soothes you when you have a cold — cough drops, tissues, tablets — like you carry an umbrella to prevent rain. (Yes, you can get those items there, but Murphy's Law applies and you'll need them when the stores are closed. Besides, they have odd cough-drop flavors.)

Taking off

Check your baggage through to your destination if it's possible (and it isn't, if you have to change airports in New York). That way it's more likely to catch up with you in Europe if it should go astray on the first leg of the trip.

The flight to Europe

The trip over is an all-night party: drinks, dinner, duty-free shopping, movie, 15 minutes of lights out for sleeping, breakfast, and then placing your seat backs and tray tables in their full upright and locked position and making sure that your seat belt is securely fastened in preparation for landing. (At that announcement, at least three persons will go to the lavatories.)

Some authorities recommend eating lightly if at all, avoiding alcohol, and trying to sleep. On one trip I turned down the free drinks and skipped coffee with dinner, and I think I felt very slightly more alert the next day. I think it's easiest to take whatever comes and try to get a nap that first afternoon.

In the morning you may be offered a hot towel. Instead, go to the lavatory and shave or put on fresh makeup — you'll feel more like it's really morning. Fresh underwear helps, too, but it requires some contortion in the usual airplane lavatory.

NOW YOU'RE THERE

Jet lag

Jet lag is a well-publicized malaise. It is basically a conflict between your inner clock and the clocks that run the world around you. Your plane took off at 7 p.m. and the flight took 8 hours. Your inner clock reads 3 a.m., but Vienna is bustling and the sun is high in the sky.

Your major difficulty is not jet lag but a night with no bed and probably no sleep. Check into the hotel and lie down for an hour or two, but no more than that. Then get up, have some lunch, go out and explore, eat dinner, and go to bed. (Europeans eat dinner later than many of us do — seven is probably about as early as you can get dinner.)

You won't sleep well the first two or three nights. Your body and your mind are at least six hours out of sync, you're in an unfamiliar bed, and fresh air comes with street noise. Someone once told me that lying down is 80 percent as good as sleeping, and after a night of horizontality you should be in good shape — or at least feel better than you did after the overnight flight.

Steve Forsyth offers a suggestion for dealing with jet lag. It condenses to: The day before you leave, load up on carbohydrates. On departure day eat nothing and drink only fruit juices, vegetable juices, and water. On the plane set your watch ahead to the new time, get comfortable, and try to sleep. When morning comes, go to the lavatory and do as many of your morning things as possible. Eat the breakfast that's offered, then after landing have a genuine breakfast and keep going all day.

Forsyth's theory is that you set your inner clock by the food and drink you put into your body: coffee and corn flakes tell your body it's 7:00 a.m.; a tuna sandwich, noon. If you eliminate these clues, the body goes on hold till it gets something definite, like coffee and a croissant.

I haven't tried his suggestions, because departure day for me usually means an early flight from Milwaukee, an airport-to-airport transfer in New York, and several hours of greeting tour members and introducing them to each other. I need food and coffee for that. It might be worth a try, though.

Other recent studies on jet lag say that exposure to sunshine helps your body adjust to the new time. I agree. My only transatlantic trip that resulted in real jet lag took off from Paris after sunset, spent 8 hours flying through the darkness, and landed at Chicago with about 8 hours of darkness to go before sunrise. For most of the next week I felt disoriented.

On the trip to Europe, give your body a subliminal message that it's morning by watching the sun rise. The flight attendant may hiss at you to put the shade down so people can sleep, but in 15 minutes she's going to turn the lights on and bring around the frozen orange juice and the pink yogurt.

On the trip home you pretty much keep up with the sun and your body, slightly bewildered, asks "You mean it's *still* 2 p.m.?" You get a meal soon after takeoff and a snack over Newfoundland. You get home at the end of the day, and your body agrees that it's the end of the day.

Hotels

The hotel rates are taken either from the 1996/97 edition of *Hotels in Austria*, available from Austrian National Tourist Offices, or from information received directly from the hotel. Rates are published here only for information and general guidance; they are not guaranteed.

Hotel reservation letters are covered in the section on language. Telephone and fax numbers are included if you should want to telephone or fax for reservations. The international dialing code for Austria is 43. If you're calling from within Austria, substitute a 0 for the 43, like we dial 1 before long-distance calls. Austrian telephone numbers don't all have the same number of digits.

Hotel rooms are usually small, probably on the assumption that when you're in them you're asleep. They are shy on light, both for reading in bed and for shaving or applying makeup. On the bed you are likely to find a down comforter instead of top sheet and blanket. In the summer and well into the fall it will be too much. One fellow I know slips it out of its giant pillowslip and uses that as a cover. Remember the comforter when you pack whatever you wear to bed, and if you normally don't, you might bring along pajamas for nights when the comforter is too warm, but nothing at all would be too cold.

In the bathroom you are not likely to find a washcloth. Often a packet of liquid soap-and-shampoo substitutes for a bar of soap (it works well for washing a shirt, if you suddenly discover you have been prodigal with clean clothing). Pack a washcloth and a small bar of soap, if those are your preferences.

Electricity is 220 volts, 50 Hertz. Keep that in mind if you are bring along an electric hair dryer (I need only a small towel for drying my hair).

In your room in the better hotels you may find a minibar, a small, well-stocked refrigerator. Write on the slip what you drink, and it will be added to your bill. It's semi-honor system — they ask what you've had, but they can easily check when they restock.

Breakfast is included in the room rate. It's usually coffee, rolls, butter, and jam, and sometimes cold meat and cheese.

Restaurants

Beware of restaurants on the tourist circuit. In August 1989 I ate three dinners at the world-famed Goldener Adler Restaurant in Innsbruck. I got the impression it was riding on reputation, as did others in the group. Perhaps you should look for places where the locals eat, where you'll have to order in German or point at what the people at the next table are eating.

Coffee is quite expensive because it is heavily taxed. I think a bunch of Austrians should dress up as Indians (either Sioux or Calcutta — it probably wouldn't matter) and fling a symbolic kilogram of coffee into the Enns or the Donau.

Sometimes you may have to be quick to say you want black coffee — quicker than I was on several occasions. You may be offered coffee "mit Schlag" or "Schlagobers" — that's whipped cream. Verlängerter coffee has been diluted somewhat and may arrive in a larger cup. If you aren't the kind of person who likes coffee that needs a knife and fork, verlängerter may be what you're looking for.

The word "menu" means the special of the day — Tagesmenu is the special meal of the day, and Tagesteller is the plate special. If you want something to read before ordering, ask for "die Speisekarte."

For estimating purposes, in October 1997 my lunches averaged 85 schillings ($6.75) and dinners 250 schillings ($19.50). A plate luncheon in a dining car will run from 150 to 250 schillings, depending on what you have to drink with it.

Tipping

Fodor's guide states that most hotels and restaurants add a service charge to their bills, but even so it is customary to tip 10 percent. The phrase for "service charge included" is "Bedienung inbegriffen." The Austrian National Tourist Office advises that service charges are included, but leave some small change for the waiter or waitress (round the tab up to the next 5 or 10 schillings); add a 5 percent tip for excellent service. Porters get 10 or 12 schillings per bag plus 5 schillings tip.

Trip details 33

Souvenirs

Rule 1. Don't buy souvenirs on the first day of the trip — especially not heavy ones.

Rule 2. If you see something you want (even the first day), buy it, because otherwise you won't think of anything else for the rest of the trip. Many stores will ship your purchases home for you, if you don't want to carry them.

Austria levies a value-added tax (Mehrwertsteuer). You can have it refunded on items costing more than 1000 schillings by filling out a form when you buy the item and showing the item and giving the form to customs officials when you leave Austria.

Photographic film

Kodak film is available — same yellow box, same film. Generally the price of Kodachrome includes processing and the price of Ektachrome does not. The prepaid processing envelope isn't valid in the U. S. You'd better take as much film as you think you will need plus 30 percent.

Store and post office hours

Stores are generally open from 0800 to 1800 with a 1- or 2-hour lunch break. Most close at 1200 or 1300 Saturday. Post offices are open Monday through Friday, 0800 to 1200 and 1400 to 1700; large-city post offices are open longer. Airmailing a postcard home will cost 13 schillings — about a dollar.

AUSTRIA'S RAILWAYS

THE LINES

Now it's all pretty much Austrian Federal Railways, Österreichische Bundesbahnen, but many lines have names and nicknames. Some of the names are geographically descriptive, but a few lines are named for members of the imperial family, rather like naming the Union Pacific and Central Pacific between Council Bluffs and Sacramento the Abraham Lincoln Railroad. (Exercise for the reader: Which railroad would you name for Millard Fillmore? for Abraham Lincoln? for Nancy Reagan? Give your reasons.)

Name	End points	Table
Arlbergbahn	Innsbruck–Bludenz	A4, C950
Aspangbahn	Wiener Neustadt–Aspang	A52
Aspangbahn	Wien–Felixdorf	A72
Außerfernbahn	Reutte in Tirol–border near Ehrwald	A41, C898
Brennerbahn	Innsbruck–border at Brenner	A3, C595
Drau- und Pustertalbahn	Lendorf–Lienz–Italian border	A22a, C970, C596
Ennstallinie	St. Valentin–Kleinreifling–Selzthal	A13, C976, 977
Erlauftalbahn	Pöchlarn–Kienberg-Gaming	A12
Franz-Josefs-Bahn	Wien Franz-Josefs Bahnhof–Gmünd	A8, C990
Gailtalbahn	Arnoldstein–Kötschach-Mauthen	A67
Görtschitztalbahn	Launsdorf-Hochosterwitz–Hüttenberg	A64
Gutensteinerbahn	Wittmannsdorf–Gutenstein	A52c
Jauntalbahn	St. Paul–Bleiburg	A62
Karawankenbahn	Villach–border near Rosenbach	A22, C1320
Karwendelbahn	Innsbruck–border near Scharnitz	A41, C895
Kremstal- und Pyhrnbahn	Linz–Selzthal	A14, C975
Kronprinz Rudolf-Bahn	Leoben–Villach–Tarvisio	A6, C980, C601
Die Krumpe	Obergrafendorf–Wieselburg	A11b
Lavanttalbahn	Zeltweg–St. Paul	A62, A6
Mariazellerbahn	St. Pölten–Mariazell–Gußwerk	A11b, C994
Mühlkreisbahn	Linz–Aigen-Schläg	A14b
Murtalbahn	Unzmarkt–Tamsweg	A63, C982
Nordbahn	Wien–border near Bernhardsthal	A93, C1150
Nordtiroler Bahn	Innsbruck–border near Kufstein	A3, C890
Nordwestbahn	Floridsdorf–Retz	A94
Ostbahn	Wien–border near Nickelsdorf	A7, C1200

Pinzgauer Lokalbahn
     Zell am See–Krimml   A23, C957
Potterndorfer Linie Meidling–Wampersdorf–Wiener Neustadt A51
Rosentalbahn   Rosenbach–Klagenfurt   A66
Salzburg-Tiroler-Bahn (Giselabahn)
     Salzburg–Schwarzach-St. Veit–Wörgl A2, C960
Schneebergbahn Puchberg–Hochschneeberg   A52e, C981
Schoberpaßstrecke Selzthal–St. Michael   A14, C975
Südbahn   Wien–Bruck an der Mur–Graz–Spielfeld
                A5, C980, C1315
Tauernbahn   Schwarzach-St. Veit–Spittal-Millstättersee
                 A22, C970
Vorarlberger Bahn Bregenz–Bludenz   A4, C950
Vorarlberger Bahn Feldkirch–Liechtenstein border near Tisis A4, C950
Vorortlinie   Wien Hütteldorf–Penzing–Heiligenstadt A10a
Westbahn (Kaiserin-Elisabeth-Bahn)
     Wien–Linz–Salzburg   A1, C950
Wiener Verbindungsbahn
     Penzing–Meidling–Wien Nord   A9
Ybbstalbahn   Waidhofen an der Ybbs–Lunz am See,
      Gstadt-Ybbsitz   A13, 13a, C978

Principal routes

- The Westbahn (West Railway), from Wien west through Linz to Salzburg and its extensions west through Zell am See to Innsbruck, Bregenz, and Buchs, Switzerland (from Salzburg to Innsbruck most through traffic runs via Rosenheim, Germany).
- The Tauern route from Salzburg south through the Tauern Tunnel to Villach.
- The Brenner route south from Innsbruck to a junction with Italian State Railways at the summit of Brenner Pass. In conjunction with the line from Rosenheim, Germany, to Innsbruck it forms one of the major north-south routes of Europe
- The Südbahn (South Railway) from Wien southwest over Semmering Pass to Graz, and the route from Bruck an der Mur southwest through Villach to Tarvisio on the Italian border.

Connections with other countries

 The principal junctions with Deutsche Bahn, German Railway, are at Salzburg, Passau, Kufstein, and Lindau. Buchs is the junction with Swiss Federal Railways. Brenner, Tarvisio, and San Candido, on the Pustertal line, are the principal junctions with Italian State Railways. ÖBB connects with the Slovenian system at Rosenbach, southeast of Villach, and Spielfeld, south of Graz.

Hegyeshalom and Sopron are the border stations for Hungary. Gmünd, northwest of Wien, is the gateway for the Czech Republic.

TIMETABLES

The Austrian timetable, *Fahrpläne,* is not available in North America. The *Thomas Cook European Timetable* is good for a start, though. You can get it from Forsyth Travel Library — dial 800-FORSYTH.

You can buy a copy of *Fahrpläne* at any station in Austria. It costs 115 schillings. The main volume measures 4⅝ × 7 inches and ¾ inches thick (842 pages). It weighs about 11 ounces. An thin accompanying booklet shows the long-distance services but does not give times for points outside Austria. You'll need the *Thomas Cook European Timetable* for that.

The timetable numbering scheme takes some figuring. The main routes, primarily those out of Vienna, are numbered with a single digit (1 for Wien–Salzburg, 5 for Wien–Graz, and 6 for Wien–Villach, for example). Lines branching from those routes have a two-digit number beginning with the digit of the main line. Branches out of St. Pölten, first junction west of Wien on the line to Salzburg, are shown in tables 11, 11a, and 11b. The next junction is Pöchlarn; the single branch there appears in table 12. The branches out of Amstetten and St. Valentin are both shown in table 13 (they join eventually), and a narrow gauge line off one of those branches is in table 13a.

Austria's network of passenger trains is confusing, even untidy, compared to those of Switzerland and the Netherlands. In those countries trains run every hour from A through B and C to D and vice versa. Branchline trains originate at B and C and run every hour to E and F. Some two-pronged lines have expresses and locals running alternately to the two destinations, or city pairs alternating in through-car arrangements.

Austria's complication arises from a network of lines radiating from Wien that branch and sometimes rejoin, with cross lines and concentric lines that in places coincide with the radial lines. There is usually a through train going to where you're going, or at least a through car.

ÖBB runs hourly fast trains from Wien to Bruck an der Mur, continuing alternately to Graz and Villach, and from Wien to Salzburg, with at least half of those continuing to Innsbruck. From Villach trains may go north through the Tauern Tunnel to Salzburg, south to Venice, or west through a corner of Italy to Innsbruck. Some trains between Salzburg and Innsbruck take the

Austria's railways   37

all-Austria route through Bischofshofen and Zell am Zee; others run through a corner of Germany. Indeed, there are seven routes a train can follow between Wien and Innsbruck.

LOCOMOTIVES

Steam locomotives

Austrian steam locomotives look odd to my eyes, and I've analyzed why. The stack and smokebox usually sat well ahead of the center line of the cylinders, putting the smokebox front practically in the same plane as the buffer beam. Many Austrian steam locomotives had twin smokebox doors, with hinges on each side and a latch in the middle. We're accustomed to the stack and the cylinders lining up and a round smokebox door held shut with lugs around the circumference.

On some locomotives the face of the buffer beam was extended upward to the level of the top of the frame; on others the front of the cylinder saddle was right behind the buffer beam.

The 76-inch-drivered 2-8-4s that were the pride of ÖBB had the stack located slightly behind the cylinders. The impression of too many wheels for the length of the boiler was accentuated by the four-wheel, inboard-bearing trailing truck. The 4-8-0s looked as though the fourth driving axle was an afterthought.

Narrow gauge locomotives generally lacked full-width buffer beams, unnecessary for the center-buffer couplers used on the narrow gauge lines, and the cylinders were in full view from the front. A few narrow gauge steam locomotives remain on ÖBB's roster.

Today's motive power

In 1995 ÖBB had 737 electric locomotives, 494 diesels, 16 steam locomotives, 225 electric multiple unit cars, and 135 diesel railcars. For more detail I recommend *ÖBB/Austrian Federal Railways Locomotives and Multiple Units*, by Brian Garvin and Peter Fox, published by Platform 5 Publishing Ltd., Lydgate House, Lydgate Lane, Sheffield S10 5FH, England; ISBN 0-906579-87-2. The price was £5.95 several years ago.

Like most European railways, ÖBB numbers its locomotives by class: four digits for the class, three for the serial number within the class, and a single check digit. Steam locomotives have two- or three-digit class numbers.

The first digit of the class indicates type:
- 1 electric
- 2 diesel
- 4 electric railcars
- 5 diesel railcars
- 6 driving trailers
- 7 intermediate trailers

Electric locomotives

The second digit is
- 0-7 AC
- 8 AC-DC
- 9 DC

The classification system grew out of the steam locomotive classification system, and the second digit originally indicated standard Austrian or German locomotives versus pre-Deutsche Reichsbahn or foreign. Now it usually indicates successive developments of a locomotive type as it increases — classes 1041 and 1141, for example.

The third and fourth digits indicate the type of service the locomotive is intended for.

- 01-19 express passenger
- 20-39 heavy freight
- 40-59 mixed traffic
- 60-69 switcher
- 70-89 spare, but used for older units
- 90-99 narrow gauge

The largest class of electrics is 1042: 001-060, 501-520, and 531-707, Bo-Bo machines built between 1963 and 1977. European notation indicates whether the axles on each truck are coupled (by rods, chains, or drive shaft) — B-B, for example — or whether each axle has a motor — Bo-Bo. The differentiation is unnecessary in North America where nearly all locomotives have electric transmission with a motor for each powered axle.

Class 1043 is a Swedish Rc2 — there are 10 of them — and class 1044 is a development of the 1043. It's first cousin to Amtrak's AEM7. There are 174 members of the 1044 class.

Class 1020 are former German E94-class Co-Co units. They aren't true Crocodiles with swiveling snouts and rod drive, but they'll do. I didn't see any on my 1997 visit to Austria, and I rode through their usual territory, the Arlberg and Brenner routes.

Austria's railways 39

Diesel locomotive 2043 053-4 has a short train of Swiss-design coaches in tow at Rohr, south of Linz, on April 27, 1989.

Diesel locomotives

For diesels, the second digit is usually 0, sometimes 1. The third and fourth digits for diesels are:

- 01-19 express passenger, over 2000 h.p.
- 20-39 heavy freight, over 2000 h.p.
- 40-59 mixed traffic, 1000-2000 h.p.
- 60-64 B wheel arrangement, under 1000 h.p.
- 65-69 C wheel arrangement, under 1000 h.p.
- 70-79 D wheel arrangement, under 1000 h.p.
- 90-99 narrow gauge

About half the diesels are four-wheel or six-wheel switchers. The principal road diesel classes are 2043 and 2143, 1500-horsepower B-B diesel hydraulics. There are 76 members of class 2043, built between 1964 and 1974 by Jenbach, and 76 class 2143 units, built between 1965 and 1977 by Simmering-Graz-Pauker.

Railcars

The third and fourth digits for self-propelled railcars are:

- 01-19 express
- 20-59 local
- 60-79 baggage
- 80-89 light railbus
- 90-99 narrow gauge

Class 4010 trainsets work many express trains. They consist of a class 4010 locomotive; 7010 open second-class coach; 7110-

Diesel railcar 5047 029-3 stands at Steindorf bei Straßwalchen on September 24, 1991. Visible behind it is a four-wheel railbus.

---

100 compartment second; 7310 diner or 7110-300 buffet-second; 7110-200 part second-, part first-class compartment coach; and 6010 open first driving trailer. There are 29 such trainsets built between 1965 and 1978. Local service is run with older class 4030 and new class 4020 trainsets. Most are three-car sets with 7030 or 7020 intermediate cars and 6030 or 6020 driving trailers.

Streetcars

You'll find streetcars in Wien, Graz, Innsbruck, Linz, and Gmunden — in descending order of size. The streetcar system in Wien is extensive and complex. The Innsbruck and Graz systems are described in the sections on those cities. Linz has two lines and Gmunden one.

PASSENGER CARS

There are two general types of passenger cars. Cars for international service are built to the standard UIC design (Union International des Chemins de fer): 26.4 meters (86 feet 7 inches) over buffers and a deep arched roof. For internal services ÖBB uses a car of Swiss design that is lower and somewhat shorter than the UIC car. The UIC cars are generally of the compartment type, and the Swiss-design cars are usually open pattern. There are still some older passenger cars in service also.

ÖBB's coaches assigned to internal service are cream and red, and there are a couple of variations of that livery plus new

Austria's railways   41

light-gray-and-red paint schemes. The paint scheme for cars in international service is red with a dark gray (nearly black) window area. The first-class portion of passenger cars is usually marked by a yellow stripe over the windows in addition to the "1" next to the door. Mail cars are yellow with a dark gray window band.

Among the initials of foreign systems you may see on freight and passenger cars are:

CD	Czech Republic
CFL	Luxembourg
DB	Germany
DR	Germany (former East Germany)
DSB	Denmark
FS	Italy
HZ	Croatia
JZ	Former Yugoslavia
MAV	Hungary
NS	Netherlands
NSB	Norway
PKP	Poland
SBB-CFF-FFS	Switzerland
SJ	Sweden
SNCB	Belgium
SNCF	France
SZ	Slovenia
SZD	Russia
ZSR	Slovak Republic

RIDING THE TRAINS

To find your train in the station, look for the poster timetables. They list all the arrivals and departures in chronological order and give track number and destination or origin.

Go to the platform for your train. You may find a board showing the composition of trains, so you can stand at the location for the car you want. You open the door yourself, by turning or pulling a handle or by pressing a button. Climb aboard and find a seat. Be sure you're not taking someone's reserved seat—printed slips indicate which seats are reserved and for which segments.

Station stops may or may not be announced — and probably not in English. Compare your watch and the timetable, and look for signs on the platforms. Trains stop long enough so you can get off comfortably, but don't dawdle. Again you'll have to open the door yourself.

Advance seat reservations are advisable in first class on the Wien–Salzburg and Wien–Graz routes when travel is heavy (summer and weekends, for example), or if you want to be sure of a window or non-smoking seat. Reservations are advisable all the time on EuroCity trains

One curiosity: Some of the coaches have little signs by the windows reading "Bei Zugluft ist dieses Fenster zu schließen." My first thought was to interpret "Zugluft" as "train air," meaning air conditioning or at least forced-air ventilation. "Zug" has a dozen or so meanings — train, pull, tug, draw, draft — depending on context. In this context, "zugluft" means "draft" and the phrase means "Close the window in case of draft." Well, duh.

Eating on trains

Many trains either carry full dining cars, which offer table d'hote meals, or offer buffet service in a dining car, which means a reasonably extensive menu, if not a complete multi-course meal. The dining and buffet service is operated by the Wagons-Lits company. You can expect to pay from 150 to 250 schillings for the plate luncheon, depending on what you have to drink with it.

Some trains offer buffet service at your seat from a minibar, a little cart that comes rolling down the aisle.

Station buffets are generally good, although they tend to be smoky (most restaurants tend to be heavier on tobacco smoke than Americans have become accustomed to).

Given the buffet and dining cars, minibars, and station buffets, you're never very far from food. Those all seem preferable to the eating method advocated by so many other guidebooks — carrying a loaf of bread and hunks of salami and cheese in your knapsack or camera bag (they never explain how to get the garlic smell off your Nikon).

CITIES

AMSTETTEN

THE FASTEST TRAINS west from Wien stop at St. Pölten, 60 kilometers and 40 minutes out, and Linz, 130 kilometers and 65 minutes from St. Pölten. Halfway between St. Pölten and Linz is Amstetten, a good-sized town and a junction and terminal for ÖBB. Amstetten serves well as a base for exploring the scenic ÖBB lines south along the Ybbs and Enns rivers, the narrow gauge Ybbstalbahn, and the line along the north bank of the Donau.

Hotel

• Hotel Gürtler, Rathausstraße 13, A-3300 Amstetten; phone 43-7472-62765, fax 43-7472-68865. Single with bath, 400-700 schillings; double with bath, 640-1000 schillings.

The hotel is a 10-minute walk from the station without luggage. I suggest a taxi when you arrive and depart. It's easier to describe the route back to the station from the hotel: turn right as you leave the hotel, walk to the main street (which at that point is called Hauptplatz, the main square), turn right, and continue east to the intersection that's a block north of the station. If you kept your eyes open during the taxi ride, you should be okay. If it's lunchtime, the station buffet at Amstetten serves a very good goulash soup.

The hotel is a block north of the main line and there's a clear view of the tracks from many rooms. The room I had in October 1997 was the nicest I encountered on the trip and by far the best value. At dinnertime I looked at the menus of the hotel and the restaurant across the street and chose the hotel (both menus

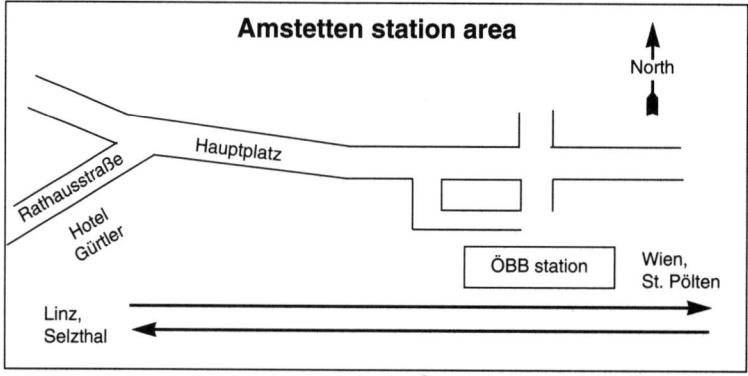

were equally enticing). The waitress asked if I'd mind sharing a table, and I said not if the other guy didn't.

I saw he was reading some tour-leader documents in English, and he spotted the Alaska Railroad pin in my lapel, and we quickly got to talking. He was leading a group of British fans on a van tour to Naples. He invited me to join them the next morning, since we were heading in the same direction, and I accepted. I got a look at a completely different sort of railroad enthusiasm — at each engine terminal the group climbed out of the van, trooped through the roundhouse and wrote down engine numbers in little notebooks, and piled back in the van.

And dinner was quite good, too.

St. Valentin

Two of the suggested itineraries pass through St. Valentin, 40 kilometers west of Amstetten. If you are in St. Valentin at lunchtime, I recommend the Gasthof zur Linde, a restaurant and hotel opposite the station (the size and malleability of the cat that lives there indicate living conditions must be okay, too).

Recommended trips

Along the Donau
Enns Valley
Mariazellerbahn
Ybbstalbahn

ALONG THE DONAU

The Westbahn, the main line west from Wien, is a high-speed double-track line (four tracks in places) parallel to the Donau (Danube) and south of it. The line is usually at some distance from the river; for a few miles west of Melk the river is visible from the train.

From Krems an der Donau west to St. Valentin a line runs along the north bank, usually within sight of the river. It's the antithesis of the Westbahn: single track, not electrified, slow. It is also very pretty, running along steep hillsides through vineyards and little towns.

The north-bank route has one named passenger train, the Rad-Tramper Wachau (Bicycle-Tramper Wachau): a diesel locomotive, a couple of coaches, and a blue-painted boxcar or two equipped for carrying bicycles. It is the only train from Wien on the route; the rest originate or terminate at Krems an der Donau. The train skips several stops in the 36 kilometers out of Krems, then settles down in the role of an all-stops local.

Amstetten	leave	0747	1313	(A1, C950)
St. Valentin	arrive	0808	1347	
St. Valentin	leave	0832	1355	(A81, C992)
Krems an der Donau	arrive	1142	1655	

Return the same way

There are several ways back to Amstetten. If you really liked the scenery and enjoy slow trains, or if the weather finally turned sunny about six minutes west of Krems, you can return by the same route. The 1735 from St. Valentin to Amstetten is an all-stops local, so you don't have worry about the speed of a mainline express making the blood rush to your head.

Krems an der Donau	leave	1418		(A81, C992)
St. Valentin	arrive	1725		
St. Valentin	leave	1735		(A1, C950)
Amstetten	arrive	1809		

Return via St. Pölten

The fastest way back to Amstetten is to go south to St. Pölten, then west on the main line to Amstetten. For lunch or dinner you could do worse than the station buffet at St. Pölten; I'd expect there's a similar establishment in the station at Krems.

Krems an der Donau	leave	1220	1702	(A11, C993)
St. Pölten	arrive	1255	1748	
St. Pölten	leave	1313	1813	(A1, C950)
Amstetten	arrive	1345	1845	

On to Wien

You can also continue to Wien and return from there. Because you have to go from the Franz-Josef Bahnhof to the Westbahnhof, I suggest this option mostly if you're moving from Amstetten to Wien. The route 5 streetcar will get you from Franz-Josef Bahnhof to Westbahnhof but it takes a while.

Krems an der Donau	leave	1150	1701	(A80, C992)
Heiligenstadt	arrive	1258	1754	
Wien FJB	arrive	1305	1800	
Wien Westbahnhof	leave	1428	1928	(A1, C950)
Amstetten	arrive	1545	2045	

ENNS VALLEY

The ÖBB line south from Amstetten (A13, C976) follows the valley of the River Ybbs through apple-growing country as far as Waidhofen an der Ybbs, crosses over a divide (and the border between Nieder-Öesterreich and Ober-Österreich), descends into the valley of the Enns, and follows the Enns south to Hieflau, then west to Selzthal. Another line follows the Enns upstream (south) from St. Valentin and joins the line from Amstetten at Kastenreith. Trains from St. Valentin continue another 3 kilometers and tie up at Kleinreifling (a few go 15 kilometers farther to Weißenbach-St. Gallen).

St. Valentin	leave	0824		(A13, C977)
Kleinreifling	arrive	0939		
Amstetten	leave	0852		(A13, C976)
Kleinreifling	leave	1006		
Hieflau	arrive	1045		
Selzthal	arrive	1130		
Selzthal	leave	1227	b1428	
Hieflau	leave	1310	1512	
Kleinreifling	arrive	1351	1552	
Amstetten	arrive	1505	1708	
Kleinreifling	leave	1418	1618	
St. Valentin	arrive	1541	1741	

b — except Saturdays

Eisenerz line

At Hieflau, well into the mountains, the Eisenerz line diverges to the southeast. The line used to be known for trains of iron ore pulled by enormous steam rack engines (2-12-2Ts), but the iron ore traffic disappeared in 1986.

A museum railroad, the Erzbergbahn, operates two passenger trains each Sunday from late June to mid-September, leaving Vordernberg Markt at 1020 and 1445 and Eisenerz at 1310 and 1550. Round trip fare on the Erzbergbahn is OS 180. For further information write the Erzbergbahn at Postfach 7, A-8794 Vordernberg. The logical way to approach the Erzbergbahn is from the other end, from Leoben — see the schedules in the section on Bruck an der Mur.

As did the previous issue, the 1998-1999 issue of *Fahrpläne* notes that the 15-kilometer Hieflau-Eisenerz section (table A13b) is about to be shut down, so check a current timetable before you try riding the branch to Eisenerz (there's no Sunday service). The Vordernberg Markt–Leoben section (table A61) appears secure.

Selzthal

The mountain scenery between Hieflau and Selzthal is as good as anything in the Canadian Rockies. The valley opens out as it nears Selzthal. A reader of a previous edition of this guide cites the station buffet at Selzthal, with chairs and tables on the platform; he also mentions a footbridge over the adjacent freight yard. Should you want an alternate route back to Amstetten and St. Valentin, take the line from Selzthal north to Linz (tables A14 and C975). It has hourly trains alternating between locals and expresses. From Linz there are frequent trains to St. Valentin and Amstetten.

MARIAZELLERBAHN

The electrified, narrow gauge Mariazellerbahn is described in the section on St. Pölten, page 74. The early departure from St. Pölten requires an even earlier departure from Amstetten, and I give the schedule by way of information, not recommendation.

Amstetten	leave	0639	0916	(A1, C950)	
St. Pölten	arrive	0713	0948		
St. Pölten	leave	0725	1025		
Mariazell	arrive	1000	1303		
Mariazell	leave	1057	1325	1552	1700
St. Pölten	arrive	1325	1608	1825	1926
St. Pölten	leave	1338	1613	1839	2013
Amstetten	arrive	1420	1645	1926	2045

YBBSTALBAHN

Running 54 kilometers south and east along the River Ybbs is ÖBB's 760mm gauge Ybbstalbahn. The line was proposed in 1893. Construction got under way at Waidhofen an der Ybbs in 1895, and by the end of 1898 the line reached beyond Lunz am See, the present terminus, to Kienberg-Gaming, at the end of a standard gauge line from Pöchlarn (table A12). A short branch from Gstadt to Ybbsitz opened in 1899. The Lunz am See–Kienberg-Gaming stretch closed in 1988 and it is now operated by a museum railroad.

You'll find the gray-and-red diesel cars of the Ybbstalbahn behind the Waidhofen station. As you board, look for destination signs. The line has a 6-kilometer branch to Ybbsitz from Gstadt, 6 kilometers out of Waidhofen, and trains divide there. Usually the forward car goes to Lunz, 54 kilometers from Waidhofen, and the rear car to Ybbsitz. (You can make a round trip from Waidhofen to Ybbsitz in about an hour.)

The train starts out by crossing Waidhofen on a viaduct. It's a pretty town and with a little time and footwork you could get pictures of trains on the viaduct.

The line follows the valley of the Ybbs River. The Ybbs is not a rushing mountain torrent, and the ride is more pretty and pleasant than spectacular — at times it seems like a park railroad. At Waidhofen and one or two other points on the line I saw freight and passenger cars, implying occasional operations with locomotives and cars instead of diesel railcars.

When I rode, I had only a few minutes at Lunz am See, and I used the time to do what I couldn't do on the diesel car. Be warned that the cars lack toilets.

Amstetten	leave	0852	*1252	(A13, C976)
Waidhofen a. d. Ybbs	arrive	0920	1320	
Waidhofen a. d. Ybbs	leave	0947	1324	(A13a, C978)
Lunz am See	arrive	1118	1457	
Lunz am See	leave	a1146	k1217	*1636
Waidhofen a. d. Ybbs	arrive	1320	1351	1813
Waidhofen a. d. Ybbs	leave	1329	1434	1835
Amstetten	arrive	1357	1505	1906

a — Monday through Friday

k — Saturday only

* — For the afternoon trip shown, weekend schedules allow later departures from Amstetten and Waidhofen or an immediate turn-around at Lunz am See.

Many trains on this route run weekdays only, weekends only, or Saturdays that are not holidays. Check the timetable footnotes carefully.

The museum line from Lunz am See to Kienberg-Gaming operates Saturdays and Sundays on the last weekend in May, the second and fourth weekends of June, and from mid-July through September (according to a 1996 schedule). Connections at both ends are reasonable, if not immediate. For information, write to the Österreichische Gesellschaft für Lokalbahnen, Postfach 625, A-1150 Wien, or fax a request to the Tourismusverband Ötscherland, 43-7416-53087.

BISCHOFSHOFEN

BISCHOFSHOFEN IS A RAILROAD JUNCTION and market town about 54 kilometers south of Salzburg on the Salzach River. It is a good base camp, and it should cost less to stay there than in Salzburg. Baedeker cites the frescoes in two churches.

Hotels

• Schützenhof, A-5500 Bischofshofen; phone 43-6462-2253. Single room with toilet and shower, 280 schillings (April 1989).

Leave the station and climb the stairs or follow the driveway up to the main street. Turn left (south) and follow the street around a curve to a somewhat wider area. Turn right (it's the first street on the right south of the station), zigzag between a couple of buildings, and the Schützenhof is the big building on the left side of the street. It's about 5 minutes' walk from the station. The food in the hotel dining room is quite good.

When I stayed there in 1989, I encountered the local choral society rehearsing. They invited me to sing along, and we had several beers afterward. May your stay in Bischofshofen also include the title song from *Oklahoma!* — in German.

• Gasthof Alte Post (∗∗∗), phone 43-6462-2307, fax 43-6462-264637. Double with bath, 740-860 schillings; single with bath, 460 schillings). It's across the street from the Schützenhof.

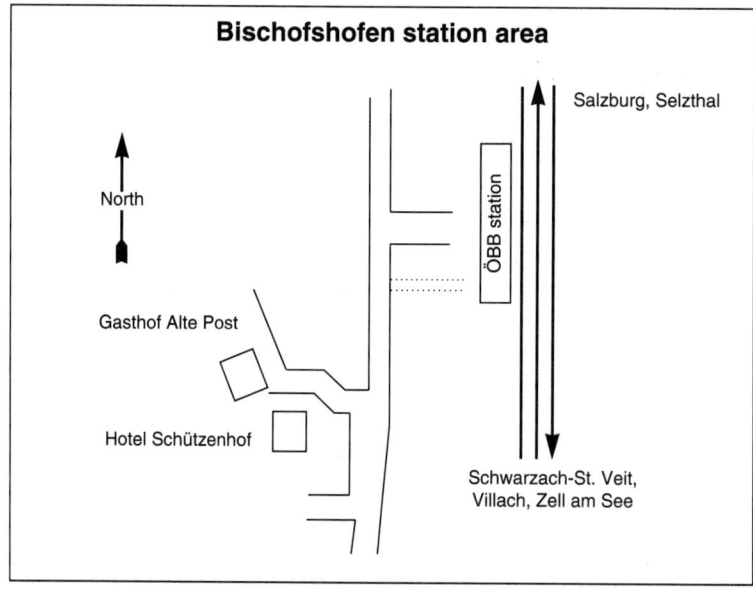

Recommended trips
Salzburg
Salzkammergut circle
Tauern Tunnel
Zell am See and Krimml

SALZBURG

For all its connection with Mozart, Salzburg is also a good railfan spot. See page 78. Trains run at least once an hour between Bischofshofen and Salzburg. Expresses take 40 minutes; locals, an hour (tables A2 and C960).

SALZKAMMERGUT CIRCLE

The circle trip through Attnang-Puchheim and Stainach-Irdning described in the section on Salzburg can also be made from Bischofshofen.

Clockwise

Bischofshofen	leave	0811	1012	(A2, C960)
Salzburg	arrive	0855	1055	
Salzburg	leave	0910	1110	(A1, C950)
Attnang-Puchheim	arrive	0956	1156	
Attnang-Puchheim	leave	1012	1210	(A17, C965)
Gmunden	arrive	1029	1224	
Gmunden	leave	1033	1225	
Hallstatt	arrive/leave	1141	1333	
Stainach-Irdning	arrive	1237	1428	
Stainach-Irdning	leave	1242	1442	(A14, C960)
Bischofshofen	arrive	1353	1553	

Counterclockwise

Bischofshofen	leave	0809		(A14, C960)
Stainach-Irdning	arrive	0936		
Stainach-Irdning	leave	1047		(A17, C965)
Bad Aussee	arrive	1122		
Bad Aussee	leave	1202		
Hallstatt	arrive/leave	1219		
Gmunden	arrive	1329		
Gmunden	leave	1330	1533	
Attnang-Puchheim	arrive	1346	1550	
Attnang-Puchheim	leave	1403	1603	
Salzburg	arrive	1450	1650	
Salzburg	leave	1505	1705	
Bischofshofen	arrive	1550	1750	

TAUERN TUNNEL

The Tauern Railway is one of Europe's major north-south routes. It follows the Schwarzach River south to Schwarzach-St. Veit. It climbs the east wall of the valley to a step in the valley, then crosses to the west wall to Badgastein. A second track has recently been added. As you travel the line you'll understand why initial proposals for this line specified a cog railway.

A plaque on the station building at Badgastein states that his most apostolic majesty, Kaiser Franz Josef I, on September 20, 1905, the line from Schwarzach to Bad Gastein were most graciously pleased to solemnly open. He became plural in the process, or at least rated a plural verb form (royalty and editors often do).

Tauern Tunnel

The 8.5-kilometer Tauern Tunnel lies between Böckstein and Mallnitz. Auto-ferry trains shuttle through the tunnel, because there's no highway for some distance east or west, and the tunnel offers the lowest crossing of the Central Alps.

The tunnel was holed through in 1907 and the southern portion of the line was opened in 1909. The northern portion of the line, from Schwarzach St. Veit to Mallnitz, was electrified in 1933, and the southern portion to Spittal in 1935.

The southern portion of the line, from Mallnitz down to Spittal-Millstättlersee, is equally scenic — the line is on the east or north wall of the valley at that point, and the views are grand.

Bischofshofen	leave	1000	(A22, C970)
Mallnitz-Obervellach	arrive	1104	
Spittal-Millstättersee	arrive	1133	
Villach	arrive	1200	
Villach	leave	1400	
Spittal-Millstättersee	leave	1427	1227
Mallnitz-Obervellach	leave	1501	1301
Bischofshofen	arrive	1600	1400

ZELL AM SEE AND KRIMML

The 760mm gauge line from Zell am See to Krimml is ÖBB's Pinzgauer Lokalbahn. The line was planned in 1889 to link the market town of Zell am See with the Oberpinzgau region. Narrow gauge was chosen for reasons of economy, and the line opened in 1898. Income didn't meet expectations, and the government had to take it over in 1906. Diesels first appeared in the 1930s, and regular steam operation ended in 1961. Steam still

An eastbound standard gauge train arrives Zell am See on August 12, 1989. The Lionel-looking track in the foreground is dual gauge, accommodating both standard gauge (1,435 millimeters as they figure it) and narrow gauge (760 millimeters).

---

operates on summer Sundays, leaving Zell am See at 0935 and Krimml at 1547. For information on steam, write to GE Pinzgau Bahn, Brucker Bundestr. 21, A-5700 Zell am See.

In 1986 Austrian Federal Railways and the province of Salzburg agreed to keep the railway in operation for another 10 years. Competing ÖBB bus service was dropped, and new marketing ideas were tried.

At Zell am See you will find the narrow gauge train on a stub track east of the the station. The line follows the broad, relatively flat valley of the Salzach River — it's not mountain railroading. About midway along the line is the winter sports center of Mittersill, the only major town along the way.

Just beyond the end of the line at Krimml is the highest waterfall in Europe (less than two miles' walk from the station to the falls; there is an admission charge).

A bus runs between Krimml and Mayrhofen, southern terminal of the 760mm gauge Zillertalbahn from Jenbach. Eastbound bus times are also shown for Zell am Ziller, where you can make a quick connection from the Zillertalbahn.

Bischofshofen   53

Clockwise

Salzburg	leave	0705		0905	(A2, C960)
Bischofshofen	leave	0756		0956	
Zell am See	arrive	0841		1041	
Zell am See	leave	849		1049	(A23, C957)
Mittersill	arrive	943		1143	
Krimml	arrive	1023		1223	
Krimml	leave	1055		1400	bus (C957)
Zell am Ziller	arrive	1205		1513	
Mayrhofen	arrive	1222		1530	
Mayrhofen	leave	1240	s1247	1540	(A31, C955)
Zell am Ziller	leave	1253	1305	1553	
Jenbach	arrive	1335	1402	1635	
Jenbach	leave	1345	1545	1745	(A2, C960)
Bischofshofen	arrive	1605	1805	2005	
Jenbach	leave	1350	1550	1750	(A3, C950)
Salzburg	arrive	1529	1729	1929	

s — steam powered, operates May through October

Counterclockwise

Salzburg	leave		0831	1031	(A3, C950)
Jenbach	arrive		1009	1209	
Bischofshofen	leave		0756	0956	(A2, C960
Jenbach	arrive		1014	1214	
Jenbach	leave		1022	1222	
Zell am Ziller	arrive		1106	1306	
Zell am Ziller	leave		1112	1327	bus (C957)
Krimml	arrive		1225	1515	
Krimml	leave	a1155	1337	1537	(A23, C957)
Mittersill	leave	1248	1417	1617	
Zell am See	arrive	1348	1510	1710	
Zell am See	leave	1424	1519	1719	(A2, C960)
Bischofshofen	arrive	1518	1605	<u>1805</u>	
Salzburg	arrive	1621	1655	1855	

a — Leaves at 1137 on Saturdays and Sundays during certain periods. Read the footnote carefully or ask the station agent or the conductor.

54 **The Railfan Guide to Austria**

BRUCK AN DER MUR

ABOUT 160 KILOMETERS (100 miles) out of Wien on the Südbahn, down at the foot of the south slope of Semmering Pass, is Bruck an der Mur. It's a railroad town. It is the junction of the Südbahn with the Kronprinz Rudolf-Bahn to Villach. There are two junctions just west of Bruck: Leoben, 16 kilometers west, where the former Eisenerz line diverges north, and St. Michael, 12 kilometers farther, where the line to Selzthal and Bischofshofen diverges. St. Michael lies off the main line; Bruck–Villach trains stopping there pull in around one side of a wye, reverse, and depart out the other side of the wye.

Several rivers join at Bruck. The Mur flows in from the southwest and turns sharply to the south toward Graz; the Mürz comes down off Semmering Pass; and the Laming joins the Mürz just north of Bruck.

"Bruck" means bridge, and students of German will remember (well, okay, *may* remember) that "an" takes the dative when it is used for postion rather than motion, and therefore "Mur" is (dem, der, dem, den) feminine. However, an unspecified river, "Fluß," is masculine.

Hotel

• Schwarzer Adler, Mittergasse 23, A-8600 Bruck/Mur; phone 43-3862-56661, fax 43-3862-56661-30. Double with bath, 890 schillings; single with bath, 500 schillings.

It's a 6-minute walk from the station to the hotel. Come out the front of the station and head straight down Bahnhofstraße,

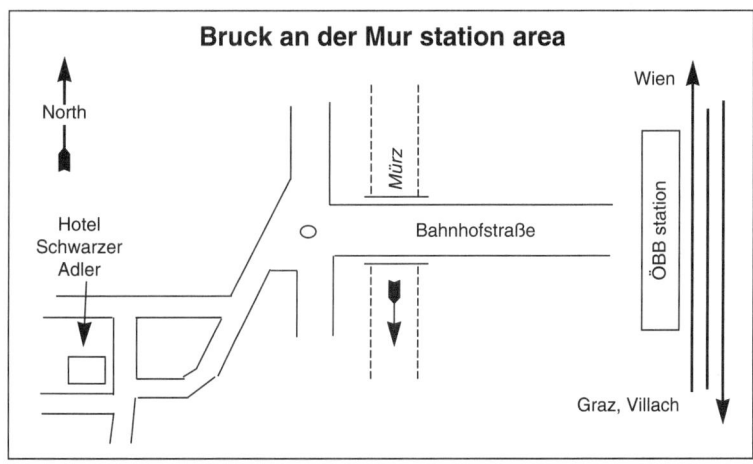

Bruck an der Mur

which crosses the Mürz, then passes under a highway viaduct. Cross one street and head diagonally to the left into an area of one-way streets. (A taxi from the station will cost you 40 schillings, a bit over $3.) I can't recall now if the hotel sign had a black eagle on it, but that's what the name would imply.

The hotel is the upper floors of a building that includes various commercial establishments on the ground floor. You'll have to take the stairs up to the office, but later you can use your room key to operate the elevator. My room was pleasant and comfortable and had a little balcony overlooking a fountain.

Dinner

I asked the proprietor if the cafe and bar in the hotel served dinner, but he said no, only "toast and snakes." I quickly remembered a sightseeing guide in Lausanne, Switzerland, who as the bus rolled through the zoo pointed out a building that housed "snacks and crocodiles." I walked through the pedestrian zone to the west of the hotel in search of dinner and fetched up at the Stadtkeller, where I dined very well on pork medallions with gorgonzola sauce for about $19. The hotel served a good breakfast, and I saw no reptiles on the buffet.

Recommended trips

Erzbergbahn
Graz-Köflacher Bahn
Murtalbahn
Semmering Pass

ERZBERGBAHN

Until 1978 enormous steam rack locomotives of the 2-12-2T type pulled and pushed heavy trains of iron ore on the line between Eisenerz and Vordernberg Markt, the steepest standardgauge line in Austria — 7.1 percent.

The Erzbergbahn now operates two passenger trains on Sundays from late June to mid-September. Round trip fare on the Erzbergbahn is 180 schillings. For further information write the Erzbergbahn at Postfach 7, A-8794 Vordernberg. These Erzbergbahn schedules are from 1997.

Bruck an der Mur	leave	0930	1306	(A6, A14)
Leoben	arrive	0941	1317	
Leoben	leave	§0950	1407	(A61)
Vordernberg Markt	arrive	1017	1434	
Vordernberg Markt	leave	*1020	*1445	Erzbergbahn

56 The Railfan Guide to Austria

Eisenerz	arrive	1135	1548
Eisenerz	leave	1310	1550
Vordernberg Markt	arrive	1415	1643
Vordernberg Markt	leave	1548	1645
Leoben	arrive	1612	1712
Leoben	leave	1643	1737
Bruck an der Mur	arrive	1654	1750

* Trains wait for the arrival of the connecting ÖBB trains
§ — Sunday only

GRAZ-KÖFLACHER BAHN

The Graz-Köflacher Bahn is primarily a coal railroad, but it also runs local passenger trains approximately hourly with diesel cars. The line runs south from Graz through Lieboch to Weis-Eibiswald; a branch runs west from Lieboch to Köflach. Schedules are different on weekends.

Bruck an der Mur	leave	0803	1201	(A5)
Graz Hbf	arrive	0837	1235	
Graz Hbf	leave	0906	1311	(A55)
Wies-Eibiswald	arrive	1025	1430	
Wies-Eibiswald	leave	1033	1448	
Lieboch	arrive	1135	1547	
Lieboch	leave	1136	1608	
Köflach	arrive	1205	1639	
Köflach	leave	1300	1734	
Graz Hbf	arrive	1350	1827	
Graz Hbf	leave	1405	1830	
Bruck an der Mur	arrive	1452	1915	

MURTALBAHN

The Murtalbahn is a division of the Steiermärkische Landesbahnen (Styrian Provincial Railway, StLB). The 760mm gauge line follows the River Mur west from Unzmarkt to Tamsweg, 64 kilometers. Most of the service is operated with diesel railcars built in the early 1980s. Painted red, green, and white, they look far more Italian than Austrian. On the property are diesel and steam locomotives, and in October 1997 an active-looking mail car was parked at Tamsweg. Trains run Monday through Saturday. On Sunday buses substitute for the trains

The lower part of the line, from Unzmarkt to Tamsweg, is relatively flat and open. The train moves along at decent speed (though it's not like a Zephyr going through Downer's Grove).

Operating headquarters are at Murau-Stolzalpe. Above

The 1215 train from Unzmarkt rolls toward Tamsweg, passing the 1340 from Tamsweg at Kendlbruck on October 17, 1997.

Murau the valley is narrower and the river is rockier, and you get the impression that this is what the Sandy River & Rangeley Lakes would be like today.

The train makes two stops in Tamsweg: Tamsweg-St. Leonhard at the lower end of town (which is where the school kids board the 1340 train) and Tamsweg, at the end of the line. It's about a 5-minute walk from Tamsweg station into the center of town, where you can find lunch.

Steam operates between Murau and Tamsweg on Tuesdays, Wednesdays, and Saturdays in July, August, and early September. You can run the locomotive by making arrangements with the StLB, A-8850 Murau; phone 43-3532-2231-0.

The Austrian Rail Pass and Eurailpass aren't valid on the Murtalbahn. In October 1997 an Unzmarkt–Tamsweg round trip from to cost 228 schillings (about $18). I thought it was worth it.

Bruck an der Mur	leave	0901	1101	(A6, C980)
Unzmarkt	arrive	1002	1206	
Unzmarkt	leave	1010	1210	(A63, C982)
Tamsweg	arrive	1153	1422	
Tamsweg	leave	k1210	a1340	1645
Unzmarkt	arrive	1352	1550	1836
Unzmarkt	leave	1357	1557	1837
Bruck an der Mur	arrive	1459	1659	1950

a — Monday through Friday; leaves at 1410 mid-July to mid-September

k — Saturday only

SEMMERING PASS

From the map it appears that the most interesting part of the line over Semmering Pass is on the north ramp between Payerbach-Reichenau and the summit at Semmering. If your objective is to photograph trains on curves and bridges, I suggest making a reconnaisance trip on a northbound local, then returning to likely spots on a southbound train.

Bruck an der Mur	leave	0810	1001	(A5, C980)
Mürzzuschlag	arrive	0856	1029	
Mürzzuschlag	leave	0908	1108	
Semmering	arrive	0924	1124	
Payerbach-Reichenau	arrive	0953	1153	
Wiener Neustadt	arrive	1025	1225	
Wiener Neustadt	leave		1135	1235
Payerbach-Reichenau	leave	1007	1207	1307
Semmering	arrive	1037	1237	1337
Mürzzuschlag	arrive	1052	1252	1352
Mürzzuschlag	leave	1131	and hourly	
Bruck an der Mur	arrive	1157		

Monday through Friday, local trains run hourly between Bruck and Mürzzuschlag and between Mürzzuschlag and Wiener Neustadt. Locals run half-hourly between Payerbach-Reichenau and Wiener Neustadt. There is a mid-morning gap in the hourly pattern over the summit, and train frequency decreases in the early evening. A few trains skip a few stations, but most of the locals make all stops. Despite the gaps and the skipped stations, it's better local service than you'll find over Sand Patch or Donner (better express service, too).

GRAZ

GRAZ IS AUSTRIA'S second largest city and the capital of Steiermark (Styria). It lies along both banks of the Mur River; the older part of the city is on the east bank. It's not on the route to much of anywhere in Austria. The main line to the south crosses the border into Slovenia 47 kilometers south of Graz. An alternate route, the Aspangbahn, runs the long way around to Wien (table A52), and the Graz-Köflacher Bahn runs into the coalfields to the west and south. Bear in mind that Graz is pronounced Grahts, not Grazz.

Hotels

• Grand Hotel Wiesler (*****), Grieskai 4, A-8020 Graz; phone 43-316-9066-0, fax 43-316-9066-76. Double with bath, 2600 schillings; single with bath, 1800 schillings. The Wiesler is an elegantly refurbished older hotel on the right bank of the Mur about a mile from the station — streetcar lines 3 and 6 pass within half a block. If you want to treat yourself to a top-grade hotel, this is the one. The dining room is excellent.

I have not stayed in the other three hotels listed. I simply saw them as I went by and noted that they were relatively convenient to the station.

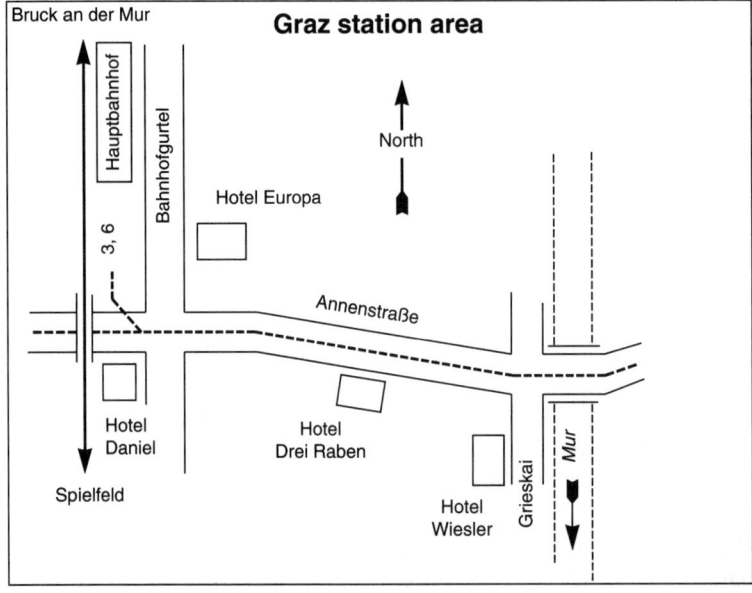

60   The Railfan Guide to Austria

• Hotel Daniel (✶✶✶✶), Europaplatz 1, A-8020 Graz; phone 43-316-911080, fax 43-316-911085. Double with bath, 1550-2000 schillings; single with bath, 1030-1530 schillings. The Daniel is south of the station at the corner of Annenstraße.

• Hotel Europa (✶✶✶✶), Bahnhofgürtel 89, A-8020 Graz; phone 43-316-9076-0, fax 43-316-9076-606; double with bath, 1540-1580 schillings; single with bath, 1100-1150 schillings. The Europa is across the street from the Daniel.

• Hotel Drei Raben (✶✶✶), Annenstraße 43, A-8020 Graz; phone 43-316-912686, fax 43-316-915959-6. Double with bath, 890-980 schillings; single with bath, 630-680 schillings. The Drei Raben is on streetcar routes 3 and 6, about halfway between the station and the river.

Streetcars

The standard-gauge streetcar system in Graz started with a horsecar system. Construction began in 1878, and it was electrified between 1895 and 1899. The streetcar company took over a meter gauge line to Maria Trost and converted it to standard

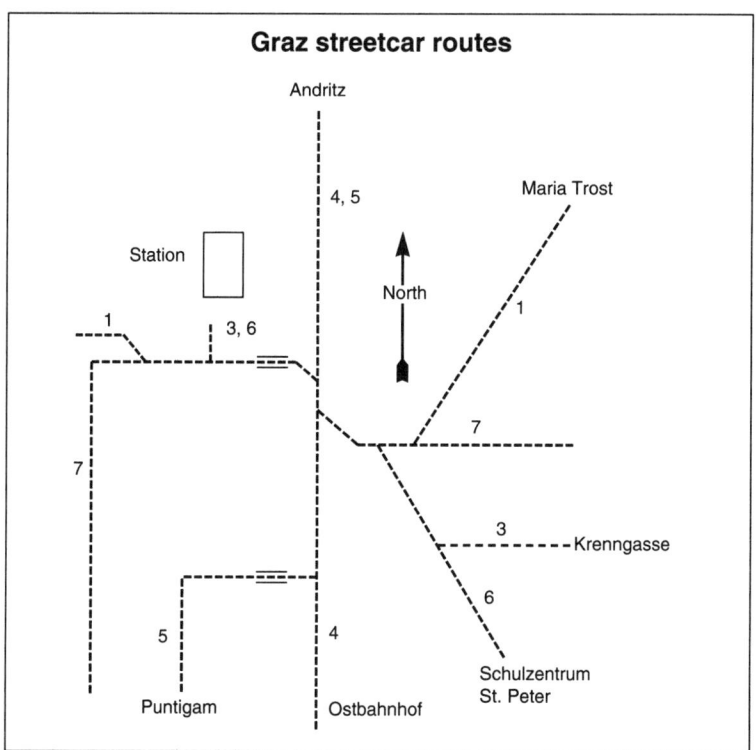

gauge in the early 1940s. The system reached its greatest extent, 42 kilometers, in 1954.

The streetcar system has six routes. All the lines run along Herrengasse between Hauptplatz and Jakominiplatz. Lines 3 and 6 begin at the station, run east along Annenstraße, cross the Mur, then follow an extremely narrow street to Hauptplatz — so narrow that if you're on the sidewalk, you'll want to pull in your stomach. Lines 3 and 6 then run south along Herrengasse to Jakominiplatz and diverge to Krenngasse and Schulzentrum St. Peter, respectively. Lines 1 and 7 originate west of the Hauptbahnhof, join 3 and 6 just south of the station, then head east from Jakominiplatz. No. 1 is the longest of the lines (10.8 kilometers) and offers a good ride. Routes 4 and 5 begin at Andritz in the north part of the city, parallel the Mur south, and part company south of Jakominiplatz. No. 4 ends a little beyond the Ostbahnhof (table 52). No. 5 turns west, crosses the Mur, and terminates at Puntigam. It's the second-longest line (9.8 kilometers).

The collection of the Tramway-Museum Graz is housed in the carbarns at Maria Trost, at the east end of Line 1, and near the Hauptbahnhof.

Other attractions

On the west side of Herrengasse, about east of the Hotel Wiesler, is the arsenal — ready for World War IV (World War III will be nuclear; World War IV will be fought with maces and halberds). It contains armor and weapons for 28,000 soldiers. North of the old part of town on the east side of the river is the Schlossberg with its clock tower. You can ride a funicular up. The views should be good.

The Austrian Open-Air Museum is at Stübing, 15 kilometers north of Graz. ÖBB has a station at Stübing; service between there and Graz is approximately hourly.

The Lippizaner horses of the Spanish Riding School spend their summers at Piber, about 40 kilometers west of Graz. Getting there requires a car or perhaps a taxi from Köflach. At Bärnbach, 5 kilometers east of Köflach, is St. Barbara Church renovated by Friedensreich Hundertwasser. It might prove to be an antidote if you've been overdosing on the baroque.

Recommended trips

Aspangbahn
Erzbergbahn
Köflach and Weis-Eibiswald
Murtalbahn

ASPANGBAHN

The main route from Wien to Graz runs southwest over Semmering Pass, then turns southward at Bruck an der Mur. A secondary route, the Aspangbahn, runs straight south from Wiener Neustadt through Aspang to Fehring, there meeting the route from Graz to the Hungarian border at Szentgotthárd. The Aspangbahn crosses and follows several rivers that flow southeastward, and on the map does a lot of twisting and turning.

There is one through train each way, the Oststeirer. It leaves Wien Südbahnhof at 0715 and reaches Graz at 1154. Returning, it departs Graz at 1625 weekdays and 1640 weekends and arrives Wien Südbahnhof at 2120. For railfan purposes, you're better off taking all-stop, second-class-only local trains, with time to take pictures as you change trains at junctions along the way.

The schedules work much better northbound than southbound. It is possible to make a trip south over the Aspangbahn, but schedules are more complicated, with different weekday and Saturday trains, and doing the trip from Graz puts you on the Aspangbahn in early afternoon — which isn't when I'm at my most alert, and probably you aren't either.

Graz Hbf	leave	0759	1004	(A52)
Fehring	arrive	0905	1112	
Fehring	leave	0911	1125	
Friedberg	arrive	1107	1308	
Friedberg	leave	1112	1312	
Wiener Neustadt	arrive	1223	1423	
Wiener Neustadt	leave	1232	1432	(A5, C980)
Graz Hbf	arrive	1437	1635	

ERZBERGBAHN

See the full description on page 56 in the section on Bruck an der Mur. Here are the connections from and to Graz.

Graz	leave	0822	1222	(A5)
Bruck an der Mur	arrive	0856	1256	
Bruck an der Mur	leave	0906	1306	(A6, 14)
Leoben	arrive	0917	1317	
Bruck an der Mur	leave	1704	1801	
Graz	arrive	1740	1835	

KÖFLACH AND WEIS-EIBISWALD

The Graz-Köflacher Bahn is primarily a coal railroad, but it also runs local passenger trains approximately hourly. The line runs south from Graz through Lieboch to Weis-Eibiswald; a branch runs west from Lieboch to Köflach. Schedules are different on weekends.

Graz Hbf	leave	0906	1311	(A55)
Wies-Eibiswald	arrive	1025	1430	
Wies-Eibiswald	leave	1033	1448	
Lieboch	arrive	1135	1547	
Lieboch	leave	1136	1608	
Köflach	arrive	1205	1639	
Köflach	leave	1300	1734	
Graz Hbf	arrive	1350	1827	

MURTALBAHN

For a complete description of the Murtalbahn, see the section on Bruck an der Mur, page 57. Instead of making a round trip from Graz, you can also ride the Murtalbahn as a side trip on the way from Graz to Villach.

A cautionary note if you do that: You can check your suitcase in the baggage room at Unzmarkt, but the interval between arriving on the narrow gauge and departing on the next ÖBB express isn't long enough for you to retrieve that suitcase, because the agent will be busy overseeing the arrival of the express. If time is important, schlep the suitcase along with you and see if you can leave it in the station during your layover in Tamsweg.

Graz	leave	0822	1022	(A5, C980)
Bruck an der Mur	arrive	0856	1056	
Bruck an der Mur	leave	0901	1101	(A6, C980)
Unzmarkt	arrive	1002	1206	
Unzmarkt	leave	1010	1210	(A63, C982)
Tamsweg	arrive	1153	1422	
Tamsweg	leave	k1210	a1340	1645
Unzmarkt	arrive	1352	1550	1836
Unzmarkt	leave	1357	1557	1837
Bruck an der Mur	arrive	1459	1659	1950
Bruck an der Mur	leave	1504	1704	2004
Graz	arrive	1540	1740	2038

a — Monday through Friday; leaves at 1410 mid-July to mid-September

k — Saturday only

INNSBRUCK

INNSBRUCK IS THE CAPITAL of the Tirol — and the Tirol is generally what you think of when you think of Austria. Innsbruck is on the tourist circuit winter and summer. The city sits on the floor of the Inn Valley, with the Northern Alps to the north and the Central Alps to the south. The Inn Valley forms a natural east-west route, and directly south of Innsbruck is Brenner Pass, leading to Italy.

Four ÖBB lines radiate from Innsbruck. The Arlberg route runs west through St. Anton and Feldkirch, entering Switzerland at Buchs after cutting across a corner of Liechtenstein. The line east goes to Schwarzach-St. Veit, Salzburg, and Munich. The Brenner route begins climbing at the south end of the station platforms and makes a fast ascent to the Italian border at the summit of Brenner Pass. Running northwest is a line that climbs the north wall of the Inn Valley to Garmisch-Partenkirchen, Germany, where it divides for Munich and Kempten via Reutte in Tirol, Austria. Trains moving between Germany and Italy and east-west trains both use the line east of Innsbruck — it's a busy stretch of track. A new bypass line has opened recently to let traffic moving between the Brenner route and the line along the Inn Valley east of Innsbruck bypass the station.

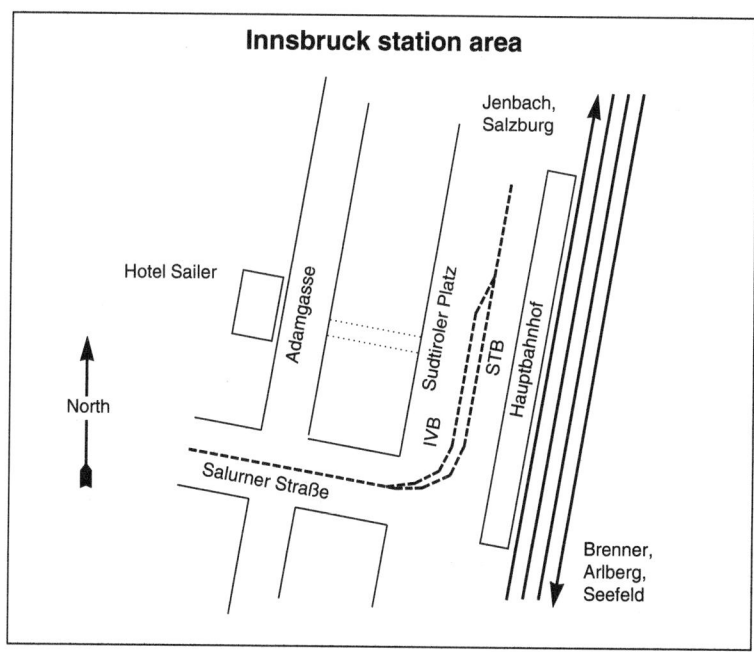

An overpass south of the station right over the junction of the Brenner and Arlberg routes offers a good view of the south throat of the station and the roundhouse.

Hotels

• Hotel Sailer (****), Adamgasse 8, A-6020 Innsbruck; phone 43-512-5363, fax 43-512-53637. Double with bath, 1600 schillings; single with bath, 1000 schillings (May-October and Christmas; 400/200 less at other times). The Sailer is only a block from the station, and it will feed you well.

• Hotel Toleranz (***), Bahnhofstraße 18, A-6200 Jenbach; phone 43-5244-2678, fax 43-5244-267814. Double with bath, 600-920 schillings; single with bath, 350-460 schillings; half-pension (i.e., dinner included) 100 schillings additional per person. The Toleranz is right behind the Jenbach station. It is closed during April, October, and November.

Jenbach is 35 kilometers east of Innsbruck. It is the starting point of the 760mm gauge Zillertalbahn south to Mayrhofen and the meter gauge Achenseebahn, a rack line to the north. Jenbach also has a car and locomotive factory.

Streetcars

Innsbruck Verkehrs Betriebe (IVB, but on the cars it looks like JVB) operates a modest meter gauge streetcar system in

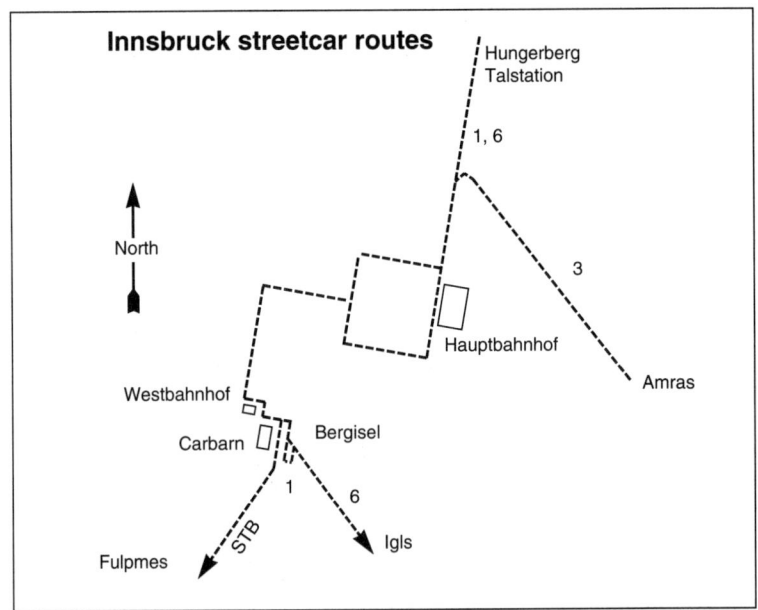

addition to its bus services. Line 1 runs from Bergisel, near the west station, through downtown to Hungerbergbahn Talstation, the valley end of a funicular also operated by IVB. Line 3, built in 1908, loops around downtown, then heads south toward the edge of the mountains. Its terminal at Amras is visible from Line 6, high above it. At the outer end of Line 3 are several cemeteries, which probably don't generate much revenue. One of them has a sign on its gate: "Ausfahrt Freihalten!" — Exit! Keep Clear! At the Rudolf-Greinz-Straße stop on Line 3 is the Rainer model railroad shop.

Line 6, which opened in 1900, is very scenic. It follows Line 1 from Hungerberg to Bergisel, then takes off on private right of way to Igls, a ski resort on the south wall of the Inn Valley. There is not much in the immediate neighborhood of the end of the car line, but a few minutes' walk will put you in the center of Igls, where you can find food and drink (and also a bus that makes the trip back to Innsbruck in about 12 minutes).

Lines 1 and 3 run on 7- or 8-minute headways weekdays and 15-minute headways late evenings and Sundays. Line 6 runs every hour on the hour from the Hauptbahnhof and takes 35 minutes. The last trip is at 1900.

You can buy streetcar tickets from the cigarette stand inside the Hauptbahnhof. A day card costs 32 schillings; a 24-hour card, 45 schillings.

There is a streetcar museum, the Lokalbahnmuseum, at the Stubaital station next to (or opposite) the Wilten basilica (a pastel rococo church). The museum is open Saturdays May through October, from 0900 to 1700. Historic streetcars run to the museum from Maria Theresien Straße at 1030 and 1430 on days the museum is open.

Recommended trips

Achenseebahn
Brenner Pass
Seefeld in Tirol
Stubaitalbahn
Villach via Lienz
Zillertalbahn

ACHENSEEBAHN

The meter gauge Achenseebahn is part rack, part adhesion, and all steam. It operates from late April or early May through most of October. It runs from Jenbach to the Achensee, largest lake in the Tirol. The line was opened in 1889, and three steam locomotives built then remain in service. A fourth was scrapped in 1945; a replacement was built recently by the Swiss Locomotive & Machine Works in Winterthur.

The train departs from the ÖBB station, immediately begins climbing, and ascends 440 meters (1,443 feet), with grades as steep as 16 percent. At Eben, 4 kilometers from Jenbach, the locomotive runs around to the front of the train to pull it the rest of the way to Achensee Schiffstation, 7 kilometers from Jenbach.

The Austrian timetable no longer includes boat schedules, but I think you can count on a connection to a boat at Achensee Schiffstation. The trip to Pertisau, the principal town on the lake, takes 15 minutes. The Fürstenhaus Restaurant, right at the dock, served a very good lunch in 1989. The boat continues north to the end of the lake. The round trip from Pertisau to the end of the lake takes about 90 minutes.

These train schedules are valid from the end of May to the end of September. Times are different and fewer trains operate during the early and late seasons.

Innsbruck	leave	0942		(A3, C950)
Jenbach	arrive	1016		
Jenbach	leave	1025		(A31a, C956)
Achensee Schiffstation	arrive	1110		
Achensee Schiffstation	leave	1105	1400	
Jenbach	arrive	1155	1440	
Jenbach	leave	1210	1500	
Innsbruck	arrive	1230	1522	

BRENNER PASS

Trains run about every hour. Expresses take 35 to 40 minutes; locals, 42 minutes — see table A3 or C595. Local trains make all stops; semifast trains stop at Matrei and Steinach in Tirol. Ride a local to some good spot and take pictures.

The line is mostly a straight shot up the pass, except for a big horseshoe curve into a side valley at St. Jodok. The line is busy and carries considerable freight. At Brenner, 37 kilometers from Innsbruck, ÖBB meets the Italian State Railways. Engines change there, since the Italian system is electrified at 3,000 volts DC (ÖBB is 15,000 volts AC).

SEEFELD IN TIROL

This line climbs the north wall of the Inn valley. It is spectacular, and the most interesting part is to Seefeld, 25 kilometers from Innsbruck. Part of the line was the scene for the final portion of the movie *Von Ryan's Express*. Your Austrian Railpass will take you 11 minutes beyond Seefeld to Scharnitz, the last station in Austria, but there's not much at Scharnitz.

The line continues past the German border at Mittenwald to Garmisch-Partenkirchen and Munich. Trains to Seefeld run about hourly. Many of the trains operate with German cars and locomotives.

Innsbruck Hbf	leave	0905	1458	(A41, C895)
Innsbruck Westbf	leave	0908	1501	
Seefeld in Tirol	arrive	0940	1531	
Seefeld in Tirol	leave	1023	1616	
Innsbruck Westbf	arrive	1054	1646	
Innsbruck Hbf	arrive	1058	1650	

STUBAITALBAHN

While the Stubaitalbahn looks like a streetcar line and is operated by the Innsbruck transit system, it is a railway with different rules and regulations. It uses double-end three-section cars (IVB's streetcars are two- and three-section single-end cars). The Stubaitalbahn is even more scenic than the No. 6 streetcar line. It runs to Fulpmes every 50 minutes from its own platform in the plaza in front of the Hauptbahnhof — see table A32. The route turns off Line 1 at the transit system's carbarn, about a block short of Bergisel, then climbs and soon offers spectacular views. The 21-kilometer trip to Fulpmes takes 59 minutes, and the car lays over 24 minutes at Fulpmes. In 1995 the round-trip fare was 68 schillings (the ticket said it was a day card).

The Stubaitalbahn opened in 1904, had an early installation of high-frequency AC electrification (2,500 volts, 42½ Hertz). It was converted to DC in 1983. The summit of the line is at Telfes (elevation 1,002 meters), 19 kilometers from Innsbruck and 413 meters above it. The line then drops to Fulpmes (936 meters). Views from the line are outstanding. The Fulpmes station buffet is open from 1200 to 1800.

Stubaitalbahn car 84 awaits departure time for Innsbruck in front of the Fulpmes station on June 16, 1995.

VILLACH VIA LIENZ

The Pustertalbahn runs east from Fortezza, on the Brenner route, through San Candido and Lienz to Spittal-Milstättersee. The schedule cited is the Pustertal/Val Pusteria, the best train on the route. There are several other trains offering only second-class cars or running at less convenient times. If you are traveling on the Austrian Railpass, you will need to buy a ticket to cover the stretch in Italy, from Brenner to San Candido. In October 1997, the fare was 128 schillings first class and 74 schillings second class.

Innsbruck	leave	1353	(A3, C596)
Brennero	arrive	1430	
Brennero	leave	1440	Ferrovie dello Stato (C596)
Fortezza	leave	1521	
San Candido	arrive	1634	
San Candido	leave	1650	ÖBB (A22a, C596)
Lienz	arrive	1731	
Lienz	leave	1739	(A22a, C970)
Villach	arrive	1850	(A22, C970)
Klagenfurt	arrive	1925	

ZILLERTALBAHN

The 760mm gauge Zillertalbahn operates most of its service with diesel cars. Trains run hourly and take about an hour for the 32 kilometers between Jenbach and Mayrhofen. About three-quarters of the route is valley-floor running, but at Zell am Ziller the scenery becomes more alpine.

A bus runs between Mayrhofen and Krimml, at the end of ÖBB's narrow gauge Pinzgauer Lokalbahn from Zell am See. Schedules are shown on page 54 in the section on Bischofshofen.

If you walk up through the village of Mayrhofen (past several restaurants) you will come to the base stations of two cable car lines. The Ahornbahn, the easterly of the two, offers wonderful views from the top, and I imagine the other does too.

In summer and at Christmas and Easter one or two trips are operated by steam locomotives. Special fares apply. You can hire a steam locomotive and run it yourself. Write to Zillertalbahn, Austrasse 1, A-6200 Jenbach; fax 43-52 44-60 6 39.

Regular trains

Innsbruck	leave	942	1342	(A3, C950)
Jenbach	arrive	1016	1416	
Jenbach	leave	1022	1422	(A31, C955)
Mayrhofen	arrive	1118	1518	
Mayrhofen	leave	1140	1540	
Jenbach	arrive	1235	1635	
Jenbach	leave	a1240	a1640	
Innsbruck	arrive	1316	1716	

a — Monday through Friday; there are plenty of other trains on the weekends

Zillertalbahn steam trains

Innsbruck	leave	942	1342	(A3, C950)
Jenbach	arrive	1016	1516	
Jenbach	leave	1047	1452	(A31, C955)
Mayrhofen	arrive	1210	1610	
Mayrhofen	leave	1247	1647	
Jenbach	arrive	1402	1802	
Jenbach	leave	1410	1815	
Innsbruck	arrive	1430	1835	

ST. PÖLTEN

ST. PÖLTEN, the capital of Lower Austria, is 60 kilometers west of Wien on the Westbahn, the main line to Salzburg. The main reason for railfans to stay in St. Pölten is the Mariazellerbahn.

Hotels
• Gasthof Graf, Bahnhofplatz 7, A-3100 St. Polten; phone 43-2742-352757. Come out of the station and look diagonally to your right. I had an odd room in a kind of annex. It was a bit threadbare and dark, but it was warm and clean and the bed was comfortable. Single room without toilet, with shower, April 1989, 310 schillings. At breakfast I heard a well-traveled American couple thanking the manager for a pleasant stay, so perhaps other rooms are better. Dinner in the restaurant of the Gasthof Graf was quite good.
• Austria Trend Hotel Metropol (****), Schillerplatz 1, A-3100 St. Pölten; phone 43-2742-70700-0; fax 43-2742-70700-133. Double with bath, 1550 schillings; single with bath, 980 schillings.

This is the first hotel in St. Pölten that I've seen listed in *Hotels in Austria*. Come straight out the front of the station and follow Kremser Gasse up through the center of town. After crossing the main square in the center of town you're on Schreinergasse, which intersects Schneckgasse at Schillerplatz. On the map in Baedeker it looks like about 600 meters (2,000 feet).

Recommended trips
Krems an der Donau and the Wachau
Melk
Mariazellerbahn
Wien

KREMS AN DER DONAU AND THE WACHAU
Krems an der Donau is a pleasant old town with an interesting pedestrian zone. Trains run from St. Pölten at least once per hour, taking 35 to 45 minutes. Furth-Göttweig is probably the closest station to Göttweig Abbey, a mammoth building overlooking the Donau (Danube). There is a pleasant-looking Heuriger (winery-restaurant) next to the station at Klein Wien.

When I rode from Krems to St. Pölten on a Friday in April 1989, a group of people boarded at Klein Wien. Co-workers in Vienna, they had knocked off work early to come out and taste the new wine, and they had some of it with them and they shared it and their picnic lunch with me. We all had a grand time, and my notes for the rest of the afternoon are a little vague.

The Wachau

The Wachau, the 18-kilometer stretch of the Donau upstream from Krems, is considered the most beautiful part of the river. An ÖBB line follows the north bank of the river from Krems to St. Valentin. Only a few trains make the entire trip. The ride is pretty but slow. The scenery includes steep hillsides, vineyards, and the Benedictine abbey at Melk.

A stay in a town on the Donau might be a pleasant alternative to St. Pölten. Thomas Anton, the proprietor of the Raffelsbergerhof (***) in Weißenkirchen in der Wachau, is a rail enthusiast, and that may constitute a recommendation of his hostelry. Postal code A-3610; phone 43-2715-2201, fax 43-2715-2201-27. Double with bath, 950-1300 schillings; single with bath, 650-750 schillings. The hotel is open May through November. Weißenkirchen is 13 kilometers west of Krems on the line shown in tables A81 and C992.

Counterclockwise

St. Pölten	leave	0905	1305	(A11, C993)
Krems	arrive	0940	1340	
Wien FJB	leave	0820	1255	(A80, C992)
Krems	arrive	0939	1410	
Krems	leave	0948	1418	(A81, C992)
St. Valentin	arrive	1254	1725	
St. Valentin	leave	1316	1752	(A1, C950)
St. Pölten	arrive	1424	1848	
Wien Westbf	arrive	1519	1935	

Clockwise

Wien Westbf	leave	1128	(A1, C950)
St. Pölten	leave	1213	
St. Valentin	arrive	1308	
St. Valentin	leave	1355	(A81, C992)
Krems	arrive	1655	
Krems	leave	1701	(A80, C992)
Wien FJB	arrive	1800	
Krems	leave	1702	(A11, C993)
St. Pölten	arrive	1748	

A Mariazellerbahn train rolls into Ober Grafendorf on April 28, 1989. The line is ÖBB's only electrified narrow gauge route.

MARIAZELLERBAHN

The 760mm gauge Mariazellerbahn opened from St. Pölten to Kirchberg in 1898, to Laubenbachmühle in 1905, and in December 1906 to Mariazell, 85 kilometers from St. Pölten. Freight service began then; passenger trains began running to Mariazell in May 1907. The line was extended to Gußwerk in July 1907. It has a respectable freight business, primarily lumber and wood products. The line beyond Mariazell to Gußwerk is closed but still in place.

Initially the line was worked by steam locomotives — six 0-6-2Ts. The opening of the mountain section beyond Laubenbachmühle in 1907 called for larger power, eight 0-8-0s with 4-wheel tenders supported at the front by the locomotive. However, the 2.7 percent maximum grade and the problem of smoke in the 2.4 km tunnel at Gösing presented difficulties that could be solved only by electrification. The line was electrified at 6,600 volts, 25 Hertz, and electric operation began over the entire route in October 1911.

Sixteen identical electric locomotives were constructed: C+C wheel arrangement, jackshaft-and-siderod drive, and a rating of 405 kilowatts (550 horsepower). They were originally numbered E1-E16. The locomotives were rebuilt in the 1960s with new bodies and were numbered 1099.01 through 1099.16, except for E15, which had been scrapped after a fall from a bridge.

There was a proposal to extend the line to a junction with the Semmering route and another to connect it with the line between Au Seewiesen and Kapfenberg.

The Mariazellerbahn is Austria's only narrow gauge line with a passenger train designated with an "E" in the timetable — for Eilzug, semifast, and even "semi" is stretching it in this case — the *Ötscherland*.

The shops are at St. Pölten Alpenbahnhof, 2 kilometers from the Hauptbahnhof. Winterbach is a scenic spot with a good view down to the station at Laubenbachmühle, 15 minutes and 9 kilometers away.

Wien Westbf	leave	0628	0928	(A1, A10, C950)	
St. Pölten	arrive	0711	1011		
St. Pölten	leave	0725	1025	(A11b, C994)	
Mariazell	arrive	1000	1303		
Mariazell	leave	1057	1325	1552	1700
St. Pölten	arrive	1325	1608	1825	1926
St. Pölten	leave	1330	1626	1833	1950
Wien Westbf	arrive	1418	1717	1923	2035

Trolley museum

At Mariazell is a standard gauge trolley museum, the Museumstramway Mariazell-Erlaufsee. It operates Saturdays, Sundays, and holidays in July, August, and September plus Mother's Day, Pentecost, Pentecost Monday, Corpus Christi, and October 26.

Die Krumpe

From Ober Grafendorf a non-electrified branch (table A11c) runs west 39 kilometers through Iowa-like countryside to a connection with the standard gauge Pöchlarn–Kienberg-Gaming line (table A12) at Wieselburg. The usual equipment for the line is diesel railcars of the type used on the Ybbstalbahn. I was surprised to see lettering on the car I rode stating that financing had been obtained through the Wilmington Trust Company in Wilmington, Delaware — that was my bank, long ago in my graduate-student days.

Most trains go only as far as Ruprechtshofen, 28 kilometers from Ober Grafendorf. There is little at the Ruprechtshofen station, but if you walk into town you can find food and drink.

If you absolutely must color in the Ruprechtshofen–

Wieselburg portion of the line on your map, weekday trains leaving Ober Grafendorf at 1753 and 1855 continue to Wieselburg. Both connect with trains north to Pöchlarn, where you can get a train east to St. Pölten. Except in the long days of summer, most of the trip will be after dark. The only way you can ride trains east from Wieselburg is to spend the night there and get up extremely early.

St. Pölten	leave	0725	1025	(A11b, C994)
Ober Grafendorf	arrive	0745	1045	
Ober Grafendorf	leave	0747	1047	(A11c)
Ruprechtshofen	arrive	0831	1131	
Ruprechtshofen	leave	*0911	*1211	
Ober Grafendorf	arrive	0955	1255	
Ober Grafendorf	leave	0958	1305	
St. Pölten	arrive	1018	1325	

x — Except Sunday and holidays
* — Daily

MELK

The town of Melk, 25 kilometers west of St. Pölten, is dominated by an enormous Benedictine abbey situated on a hill between the center of town and the Donau. It is worth seeing.

It's possible to photograph trains with the abbey as a backdrop. Cross to the south side of the tracks using the station footbridge, then walk west on a street that climbs up a hill and offers an excellent photo location. Westbound trains stopping at Melk are the best bet — expresses are quiet and can catch you with the shutter uncocked.

Wien Westbf	leave	0833	1245	1440		(A1, C950)
St. Pölten	leave	0922	1338	1533		
Melk	arrive	0940	1355	1551		
Melk	leave	1210	1408	1608	1813	
St. Pölten	arrive	1226	1424	1624	1831	
Wien	arrive	1319	1519	1717	1923	

Cruising down the river

Table 995 of the *Thomas Cook European Timetable* shows boat service between Melk and Krems an der Donau. The boat dock at Melk is behind the west end of the abbey; the dock at Krems is perhaps a mile west of the station (taxis are available).

With the Benedictine abbey as a backdrop, a train accelerates west out of Melk on August 5, 1989. The Donau (Danube) is just beyond the abbey.

Melk (boat dock)	leave	1100	1350	1515	(C995)
Krems (boat dock)	arrive	1230	1530	1645	
Krems (ÖBB station)	leave	1341	1620	1820	(A11, C993)
St. Pölten	arrive	1424	1655	1855	
Krems (ÖBB station)	leave	1350	1701	1950	(A80, C992)
Wien FJBf	arrive	1505	1800	2105	

WIEN

Hourly expresses depart St. Pölten at 50 past each hour, arriving at Wien's Westbahnhof at 35 past the next hour (there are locals and other express trains, too). Expresses return every hour at 20 and 28 past, arriving St. Pölten on the next hour and at 11 past. Local trains take 65 minutes. See table A1 for the express trains and table A10 for all trains.

St. Pölten 77

SALZBURG

SALZBURG IS THE CAPITAL of Salzburg Land (Salzburg Province). It is a tourist mecca, and the tourist industry is about two-thirds Mozart and one-third *The Sound of Music*. The intense competition between the two probably makes the Salzburg tourist office wish Mozart had written *The Sound of Music*.

One Mozartiana caution, by the way: I encountered large, round chocolate candies and a very heavy torte with pale green frosting, both marketed as Mozart's favorites or something like that. Neither was any great shakes. Stick with his music.

For all its emphasis on tourism, Salzburg has plenty to offer the rail enthusiast. The station is also served by Deutsche Bahn, German Railway, so it counts as a "two-fer" for train-watching purposes. Photographic opportunities aren't particularly good in the station, but just west of the station DB crosses the Salzach River on a deck girder bridge. There are promenades on both banks of the river, and it's a good photo spot.

The station tracks run northeast-southwest. Because the river and the tracks curve and the streets form neat rectangular grids in some places and not in others, you'll want to pick up a city map at the tourist information bureau in the station.

Just north of the main station, diagonally to the right as you come out, is the station of the Salzburger Lokalbahn, which operates passenger and freight service to Lamprechtshausen. The freight yard and carbarns are within walking distance.

East of Salzburg lies a salt-mining district, the Salzkammergut, now known more for its lakes and mountains than for its salt. The Salzburg–Wien main line skirts the area to the north, but the ÖBB route from Attnang-Puchheim to Stainach-Irdning and several Stern & Hafferl lines penetrate the area.

One guidebook mentions that the weather of the Salzkammergut lends it a Celtic sort of shrouded beauty and that the rain and drizzle can settle in for days. I encountered sunny weather there once and it was lovely, but after several visits I've decided that a good day in Salzburg is when you can stare at the bright spot in the sky for no more than two minutes without hurting your eyes. I wish you good luck.

Boats ply several of the lakes. The principal connecting points for train-riders are Attersee, Hallstatt station, and Gmunden. Boat connections for Hallstatt are shown on the same page of *Fahrpläne* as table 17; boat connections at Attersee are on the same page as table 18.

Hotels

Most of the hotels are up in the touristy part of town. However, opposite the station, to the left as you come out the main door, is the Hotel Europa, a tall, modern building. The Bayrischer Hof is diagonally to the right — turn right, then at the end of the plaza turn left past the Salzburger Lokalbahn station and a department store, cross a street, and you're there. I have stayed at the Bayrischer Hof and found it quite pleasant.

- Bayrischer Hof (****), Kaiserschützenstraße 1, A-5021 Salzburg. Phone 43-662-46970-0, fax 43-662-46970-25. Double with bath, 1310-1970 schillings; single with bath, 835-1200 schillings.
- Hotel Europa (****), Rainerstraße 31, A-5050 Salzburg. Phone 43-662-889930, fax 43-662-889938. Double with bath, 2160 schillings; single with bath, 1560 schillings.
- Best Western Stiegelbräu K&K Hotel (****), Rainerstraße 14, A-5020 Salzburg. Phone 43-662-88992; fax 43-662-88992-71. Double with bath, 1890-2270 schillings; single with bath, 1160-1660 schillings.

The Stiegelbräu is a bit farther from the station than the first two, about 600 meters (2000 feet, 10 minutes' walk) to judge from the map in Thomas Cook's *European Cities*. Come out of the station, turn left, and walk along the street that lies at the foot of the railroad embankment. Cross St. Julien Straße (the first underpass) and turn left at the second underpass. The hotel is just beyond the underpass. From the map it appears you could get a room with a view of the tracks.

Also approximately two blocks from the station is the

- Hotel Zum Hirschen (****), St. Julien Straße 21-23, A-5020 Salzburg. Phone 43-662-88903-0, fax 43-662-88903-58. Double with bath, 1500-1700 schillings; single with bath, 950-1050 schillings.

Turn left as you leave the station and walk along the street that lies at the foot of the railroad embankment. At St. Julien Straße (the first underpass) turn right — the hotel is just beyond the next corner (Elisabeth Straße).

Recommended trips

Gmunden, Vorchdorf, and Lambach
Salzburger Lokalbahn
Salzkammergut circle
Schafberg
Vöcklamarkt and Attersee

Gmunden streetcar No. 8, built in 1961, stands outside the Gmunden carbarn on April 22, 1989.

GMUNDEN, VORCHDORF, AND LAMBACH

At Gmunden a meter gauge streetcar operated by Stern & Hafferl meets the train and runs 2.4 kilometers to the center of town, down on the shore of the Traunsee.

Gmunden had the first electric lighting plant in Austria in 1894, and an accessory to that was a streetcar line connecting the town with the station. It is now something of a tourist attraction. It is considered the smallest streetcar system in the world, and the 9.6 percent grade on the line presses the limits of adhesion. The streetcar company even has an enthusiast group: the Verein pro Gmunder Straßenbahn, Postfach 122, A-4810 Gmunden.

Gmunden to Vorchdorf

After you ride the streetcar down into Gmunden, perhaps pausing for lunch at the little cafe a few doors west of where the car stops, walk east along the lakefront to Gmunden Seebahnhof. There you will find the meter-gauge Lokalbahn Gmunden-Vorchdorf, which will take you 13 kilometers to Vorchdorf-Eggenberg. For part of the way the line used to share track (more accurately, one rail) with a standard gauge ÖBB line.

Vorchdorf to Lambach

At Vorchdorf-Eggenberg change to the standard gauge Lokalbahn Lambach-Vorchdorf-Eggenberg for a 12-kilometer ride to Lambach, on the Salzburg–Linz main line. The two Lokalbahns are operated by Stern & Hafferl, a firm that was founded in 1883 to build and operate local railways. The company's operations today are clustered between Linz and Salzburg.

Salzburg	leave	0910	1110	(A1, C950)
Attnang-Puchheim	arrive	0956	1156	
Attnang-Puchheim	leave	1012	1210	(A17, C965)
Gmunden	arrive	1029	1224	
Gmunden Seebahnhof	leave	1300	1345	(A16b)
Vorchdorf-Eggenberg	arrive	1335	1420	
Vorchdorf-Eggenberg	leave	1425	1552	(A16a)
Lambach	arrive	1450	1617	
Lambach	leave	1507	1704	(A1)
Salzburg	arrive	1623	1823	

Lambach to Haag and return

Before returning to Salzburg you can easily make a round trip to Haag am Hausruck on yet another Stern & Hafferl line, the standard gauge Lokalbahn Lambach-Haag. The distance is 22 kilometers. A few trains in each direction run to or from Wels, a major ÖBB junction 13 kilometers east of Lambach. Almost every train in table A16c has a note about days it does or does not operate.

Lambach	leave	1515		(A16c)
Haag	arrive	1600		
Haag	leave	1605	*1714	
Lambach	arrive	1650	1800	
Lambach	leave	1704	1828	(A1)
Salzburg	arrive	1823	c1950	

* — Last train of the day out of Haag.
c — Change trains at Attnang-Puchheim.

SALZBURGER LOKALBAHN

The standard gauge Salzburger Lokalbahn, a remnant of the Salzburg streetcar system, offers a pleasant ride out to the north. The line's primary purpose is to carry coal to a power plant.

Round-trip fare was 69 schillings in 1991. Trains run every 30 minutes weekdays and hourly on Sundays (table A21). The 25-kilometer ride to Lamprechtshausen takes 35 minutes.

The only major town on the line is Oberndorf, birthplace of

Two Salzburger Verkehrsbetriebe (Salzburger Lokalbahn) freight motors head a train of covered coal hoppers at Oberndorf on June 14, 1995.

"Silent Night" and site of an interesting iron bridge over the Salzach. The bridge leads to Laufen, Germany (on the DB line from Freilassing to Mühldorf — passenger trains every 2 hours).

At Bürmoos, 2 kilometers from the end of the line, the line connects with the Salzach-Kohlenbergbau line, a Stern & Hafferl operation that runs 9 kilometers to Trimmelkam.

The carbarn and the freight interchange in Salzburg are only a few minutes' walk from the Hauptbahnhof. The current timetable says nothing about it, but in past years the line has operated antique equipment on Saturdays from mid-May through September. Check the bulletin board at the Lokalbahn station. The poster may refer to such a train as an "Oldtimer Fahrt" (I'm not making this up).

SALZKAMMERGUT CIRCLE

The Salzkammergut line from Attnang-Puchheim to Stainach-Irdning is among the most scenic in Austria.

A reader of this guide suggests two additions to the Salzkammergut circle trip. First, Selzthal, east of Stainach-Irdning, is a busy junction. There is a buffet right on the H-shaped platform, and a footbridge offers a view of the trains. There's also a small hump yard west of the station. Second, he suggests a stopover at Hallstatt, which is across the lake from its station and reached by a ferry. Hallstatt is about halfway between Gmunden and Stainach-Irdning.

At Gmunden take the time to ride the streetcar line down into town.

Clockwise

Salzburg	leave	0910	1110	(A1, C950)
Attnang-Puchheim	arrive	0956	1156	
Attnang-Puchheim	leave	1012	1210	(A17, C965)
Gmunden	arrive	1029	1224	
Gmunden	leave	1033	1225	
Hallstatt	arrive/leave	1141	1333	
Stainach-Irdning	arrive	1237	1428	
Stainach-Irdning	leave	1242	1442	(A14, C960)
Bischofshofen	arrive	thru	1553	
Bischofshofen	leave	train	1603	(A2, C960)
Salzburg	arrive	1439	1646	

Counterclockwise

Salzburg	leave	0914	1121	(A2, C960)
Bischofshofen	arrive	0957	thru	
Bischofshofen	leave	1008	1208	(A14, C960)
Stainach-Irdning	arrive	1117	1317	
Stainach-Irdning	leave	1209	1432	(A17, C965)
Hallstatt	arrive/leave	1314	1526	
Gmunden	arrive	1431	1631	
Gmunden	leave	1433	1632	
Attnang-Puchheim	arrive	1447	1646	
Attnang-Puchheim	leave	1503	1703	(A1, C950)
Salzburg	arrive	1550	1750	

SCHAFBERG

Between Salzburg and Bad Ischl is a mountain named Schafberg. A 5.8-kilometer meter gauge cog railway climbs 1,190 meters (3,900 feet) from St. Wolfgang to the summit. The railway was built by Stern & Hafferl and opened in 1893. It is now operated by ÖBB. It has 5 steam locomotives and 2 diesel cars.

The Schafbergbahn operates from May to the last weekend of October. Both *Fahrpläne* and the *Thomas Cook European Timetable* note that the Schafbergbahn runs only if at least 20 passengers show up for the train.

Getting there from Salzburg and riding it takes most of a day. You will have to change buses at Strobl. Riding the Schafbergbahn might provide a good reason to rent a car for the day.

Historical note: The Salzkammergut Lokalbahn from Salzburg to Bad Ischl was dismantled in 1957 over great protest. It had almost a Rowland Emmett mystique to it, to judge by the photos in books.

Salzburg (station)	leave	0915		bus (C962)
Strobl	arrive	1029		
Strobl	leave	1040		bus (C963)
St. Wolfgang	arrive	1055		
St. Wolfgang	leave	1110	1209	Schafberg-
Schafbergspitze	arrive	1151	1258	bahn (A17c)
Schafbergspitze	leave	1211	1328	
St. Wolfgang	arrive	1256	1413	
St. Wolfgang	leave	1314	1425	
Strobl	arrive	1329	1440	
Strobl	leave	1341	1441	
Salzburg	arrive	1455	1555	

VÖCKLAMARKT AND ATTERSEE

The Lokalbahn Vöcklamarkt-Attersee, a Stern & Hafferl meter gauge railway, runs from Vöcklamarkt, on the Salzburg–Linz main line, down through woods, fields, and villages to the lake at Attersee, 13 kilometers. It is a pleasant ride, and there are good views out front past the motorman.

Salzburg	leave	0938	1226	(A1, C950)
Vöcklamarkt	arrive	1019	1320	
Vöcklamarkt	leave	1045	1345	(A18)
Attersee	arrive	1114	1414	
Attersee	leave	1145	1445	
Vöcklamarkt	arrive	1215	1515	
Vöcklamarkt	leave	1248	1540	
Salzburg	arrive	1345	1623	

Neither the Austrian Railpass nor the Eurailpass is valid on the line. The round-trip fare from Vöcklamarkt to Attersee was 54 schillings in 1991.

Stern & Hafferl offers a pass (Umweltkarte) good on all its operations. In 1991 it cost 100 schillings for ten 8-kilometer zones. Two persons can share the card. Write to Stern & Hafferl, Kuferzeile 32, A-4810, Gmunden.

On Wednesdays in summer the 1345 from Vöcklamarkt carries a buffet car. On Thursdays in summer the 1445 from Attersee carries a children's car. It is possible to hire a motor car

A Vöcklamarkt-Attersee car once on the roster of the Aigle-Ollon-Monthey-Champéry in Switzerland pauses for passengers at St. Georgen im Attergau on September 24, 1991.

---

you can operate yourself or a buffet car. For particulars, fax a request for information to Stern & Hafferl at 43-7666-7802-16.

Boats depart Attersee for cruises along the lake at 0940, 1210, and 1440 (the trip takes 2 hours 25 minutes) and 1040, 1155, 1425, and 1540 (1 hour 15 minutes).

VILLACH

VILLACH IS THE SECOND LARGEST CITY of Carinthia, at the crossing of the Wien–Venice and Munich–Zagreb rail routes. The River Drau flows through the center of the city. In the surrounding area are a number of lakes. The Carinthia Summer Festival offers music at several different locations nearby.

Klagenfurt, 38 kilometers east, is the capital of Carinthia. I think Villach is probably more interesting in terms of topography and railroad activity. Just west of Klagenfurt is the Wörthersee, a lake lined with resort towns.

Hotels

• Hotel Mosser (✶✶✶✶), Bahnhofstraße 9, A-9500 Villach; phone 43-4242-24115, fax 43-4242-24115-222. Double with bath, 900-1400 schillings; single with bath, 600-800 schillings.

The Hotel Mosser is on Bahnhofstraße a block from the station. It has only a bar, but the Brauhof Restaurant across the street will feed you quite well. Beyond the Hotel Mosser Bahnhofstraße leads down the hill and across the River Drau to the pedestrian mall at the center of the city.

• Hotel City, Bahnhofplatz 3, A-9500 Villach; phone 43-4242 26766. It is not listed in *Hotels in Austria*, but in October 1997 it appeared to be open for business.

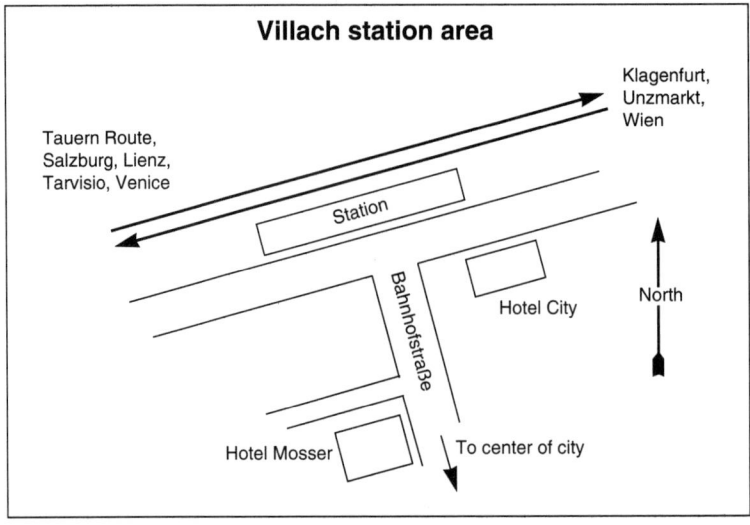

Recommended trips
Innsbruck via Lienz
Klagenfurt via Rosenbach
Murtalbahn
St. Veit an der Glan via Ossiach

INNSBRUCK VIA LIENZ

The Pustertalbahn runs west from Spittal-Milstättersee through Lienz and San Candido to Fortezza, on the Brenner route in Italy. The schedule cited is the Pustertal/Val Pusteria, the only through train on the route. Several other trains offer only second-class cars and require one or two changes of train and long layovers. If you are traveling on the Austrian Railpass, you will need to buy a ticket to cover the stretch in Italy, from San Candido to Brenner. In October 1997, the fare was 128 schillings first class and 74 schillings second class.

Westbound

Klagenfurt	leave	0636	(A6, C980)
Villach	leave	0712	(A22, C970)
Lienz	arrive	0827	(A22a, C970)
Lienz	leave	0832	(A22a, C596)
San Candido	arrive	0913	
San Candido	leave	0925	Ferrovie dello Stato
Fortezza	arrive	1035	
Brenner	arrive	1117	
Brenner	leave	1127	ÖBB (A3, C596)
Innsbruck	arrive	1203	

KLAGENFURT VIA ROSENBACH

The line between Rosenbach and Klagenfurt, 31 kilometers, the Rosentalbahn, was built as part of a route to Trieste. The major feature of the line was the Karawanken Tunnel south of Rosenbach. Now passenger trains between Wien and Italy operate via Villach, and trains between Wien and Croatia run through Graz, bypassing the Rosentalbahn.

There is a grade of 2.1 percent on the route (perhaps that is the reason through trains take other routes), and several viaducts.

You can, of course, go from Villach to St. Veit via Ossiach (table A65) and return via Klagenfurt and Rosenbach. Other lines in the area that might be worth investigating are the Gailtalbahn, which follows the River Gail west to Kötschach-Mauthen from Arnoldstein, south of Villach (table A67); the line from St. Veit an der Glan to Hüttenberg (table A64); and the alternate route from Klagenfurt to Zeltweg via St. Paul (table A62). Buses substitute for trains between Rosenbach and Klagenfurt on Saturday afternoons and Sundays.

Clockwise

Villach	leave	1120	1602	(A6)
Klagenfurt	arrive	1158	1633	
Klagenfurt	leave	1225	a1643	(A66)
Rosenbach	arrive	1304	1723	
Rosenbach	leave	1307	1805	(A22, C1320)
Villach	arrive	1340	1840	

a — Monday through Friday

Counterclockwise

Villach	leave	1022	a1410	(A22, C1320)
Rosenbach	arrive	1055	1440	
Rosenbach	leave	1125	a1530	(A66)
Klagenfurt	arrive	1203	1613	
Klagenfurt	leave	1231	a1620	(A6)
Villach	arrive	1313	1652	

a — Monday through Friday

MURTALBAHN

The closest narrow gauge line to Villach is the Murtalbahn, a division of the Steiermarkische Landesbahnen, which runs from Unzmarkt to Tamsweg. Riding the line from Villach makes a long day: It's an hour and a half or two hours from Villach to Unzmarkt, and the narrow-gauge line is two hours end to end. Consider making it a side trip as you go between Villach and Wien, Graz, or Bruck an der Mur.

A cautionary note if you do that: You can check your suitcase in the baggage room at Unzmarkt, but the interval between arriving on the narrow gauge and departing on the next ÖBB express isn't long enough for you to retrieve that suitcase, because the agent will be busy overseeing the arrival of the express. If time is tight, schlep the suitcase along with you and see if you can leave it in the station during your layover in Tamsweg.

For a full description of the Murtalbahn, see page 57 in the section on Bruck an der Mur.

Villach	leave	0812	1012	(A6, C980)
Klagenfurt	leave	0841	1041	
Unzmarkt	arrive	0956	1156	
Unzmarkt	leave	1010	1210	(A63, C982)
Tamsweg	arrive	1153	1422	
Tamsweg	leave	k1210	a1340	1645
Unzmarkt	arrive	1352	1550	1836
Unzmarkt	leave	1403	1603	1924
Klagenfurt	arrive	1518	1718	2059
Villach	arrive	1548	1748	2140

a — Monday through Friday; leaves at 1410 mid-July to mid-September

k — Saturday only

ST. VEIT AN DER GLAN VIA OSSIACH

This secondary line, which during World War I served as the main line to Italy, runs along the north shore of the Ossiacher See, then follows the River Glan out to St. Veit. Trains do not run on Sundays. Buses run a substitute service on different schedules, but that isn't what you came for.

About 8 minutes beyond St. Veit (change there; connections are good) is Launsdorf-Hochosterwitz, the station for Burg Hochosterwitz, a 16th-century castle built atop a hill. It's about a 30-minute walk from the station to the entrance to the castle.

The road up to the castle (pedestrians only) passes through 14 gates of different types as it winds around the hill, and the views are excellent. Admission is 40 schillings. There is a restaurant in the courtyard at the top.

Clockwise

Villach	leave	0815	1212	(A65)
St. Veit	arrive	0920	1317	
St. Veit	leave	0940	1340	(A6, C980)
Klagenfurt	arrive	0959	1359	
Villach	arrive	1040	1440	

Counterclockwise

Villach	leave	1120	1520	(A6, C980)
Klagenfurt	leave	1202	1602	
St. Veit	arrive	1223	1623	
St. Veit	leave	1240	1628	(A65)
Villach	arrive	1342	1740	

WIEN (VIENNA)

PEOPLE KEEP SAYING "Vienna is a *wonderful* city!" Every time I go there I agree more and more.

Hotels
- Austrotel (✶✶✶✶), Löhrgasse 3 (Felberstraße 4), A-1150 Wien; telephone 43-1-981110, fax 43-1-98111930. Double with bath, 2250 schillings; single with bath, 1700 schillings. The Austrotel is just north of the Westbahnhof; turn left as you leave the front of the station.
- Hotel An der Wien (✶✶✶), Keißlergasse 24, A-1140 Wien; telephone 43-1-942114, fax 43-1-942114-13. Double with bath, 900 schillings; single with bath, 550 schillings. The An der Wien is next to the Wien Hütteldorf station, two stops (7 minutes) west of Westbahnhof. Many through trains stop there.
- Hotel Cristall (✶✶✶), Franzenbrückenstraße 9 (a block or two south of Wien Nord station on the O streetcar line), A-1020 Wien; phone 43-1-211300; fax 43-1-2113072. Double with bath, 1200-1380 schillings; single with bath, 760-850 schillings.
- Hotel Nordbahn (✶✶✶), Praterstraße 72 (a block southwest of Wien Nord station and the Praterstern subway station), A-1020 Wien; phone 43-1-211300. Double with bath, 1080-1440 schillings; single with bath, 995 schillings.
- Hotel Reichshof (✶✶✶), Mühlfeldgasse 13 (a block north of Wien Nord station), A-1020 Wien; phone 43-1-2143178; fax 43-1-2143178-66. Double with bath, 630-1000 schillings per person.
- Hotel Stasta (✶✶✶), Lehmanngasse 11, A-1235 Liesing; telephone 43-1-86597880. Double with bath, 860-920 schillings; single with bath, 660-720 schillings; less without private bath. A friend highly recommends this family-operated hotel. It is just a few steps from the Liesing station, which is 11 kilometers and 4 stops from the Südbahnhof on the route to Wiener Neustadt (table 9) — one or two trains per hour, plus several on the suburban line to Wien Mitte and Nord.

There are two telephone codes for Wien. For international calls use 1. Within Austria use 0-222.

Other attractions
A non-railfan traveling with you can keep busy. Among the principal tourist sights are Schönbrunn Palace, the art museum, St. Stephan's Cathedral, the Spanish Riding School, and the various buildings of the Hofburg. Wien is a good city for eating and drinking. Investigate a Heuriger, which is a tavern specializing

A six-wheel diesel switcher, No. 2067 109-5, switches passenger cars at Westbahnhof on August 5, 1989.

---

in its own wine (and serving it in large pitchers). There's one in Heiligenstadt that was Beethoven's local pub, and Baedeker mentions one in Nußdorf, near the end of the D streetcar line.

Stations

The two principal rail terminals are Westbahnhof and Südbahnhof — West and South stations. The Westbahn ends at, appropriately, the Westbahnhof. It's a modern building at the corner of Mariahilferstraße and Gürtel (which means "belt"). The tracks are above street level. The principal transit connections are subways U3 and U6 and streetcars 5 and 18.

Most trains on the Westbahn stop at Hütteldorf, 6 kilometers west of Westbahnhof. Hütteldorf is the western terminus of the U4 subway line.

The Südbahnhof, at Gürtel and Prinz-Eugenstraße, has tracks on three levels, two above street level and one below. On the first level up you find trains for the east, and above that are trains for the southwest — the Südbahn. The tracks of the subterranean level connect the Südbahn to the Mitte and Nord stations.

That first level up is a lot more interesting since the fall of the Iron Curtain. You can see a lot of interesting equipment there, some of it lettered in unfamiliar alphabets.

Most trains on the Südbahn stop at Wien-Meidling, 4 kilometers out. Wien-Meidling is the busiest station in Austria. It is also served by the Wiener Lokalbahn (WLB), transit line U6 (a high-speed, high-platform streetcar line), and streetcar line 62. Meidling and Philadelphiabrücke are pretty much the same place. One stop south of Meidling on the U6 line is Tscherttegasse, the north end of which can be considered a Hot Spot, with views of the U6 line, the WLB, an ÖBB suburban line, the ÖBB line that connects Westbahnhof and Südbahnhof, and an ÖBB freight line.

Of lesser importance are the Franz Josefs-Bahnhof (FJB) and the Wien Nord station. The FJB is on streetcar lines D and 5 and a block from the Friedensbrücke station on the U4 subway line. The Franz-Josefs Bahnhof is only slightly more railfannable than Union Station, Chicago — you can walk out to the platforms unimpeded, but it's all under cover.

The first stop out of FJB is Heiligenstadt, also served by streetcar D, subway U4, and S-Bahn routes.

The Nord Bahnhof is a through station on an island formed by the Donau and the Donau Canal. It is above street level and hosts mostly suburban trains. It is served by the Praterstern station of the U1 subway line and streetcars 5, 21, and O.

Suburban trains running south from Nord stop at Mitte, underground in the center of the city. Mitte is also on the U3 and U4 subway lines and streetcar line O.

Station to station

If you take the subway to get from one ÖBB station to another, you will probably have to change trains, but the system is well marked and easy to use. Streetcars connect most of the stations above ground. The trips take longer, but you get a look at the city on the way. Between Westbahnhof and Südbahnhof take the route 18 car. Between Westbahnhof, Franz-Josefs Bahnhof, and Nord use streetcar 5. Route D runs between Südbahnhof, Franz-Josefs Bahnhof, and Heiligenstadt. Route O connects Süd and Nord. Suburban trains on routes S1, S2, and S3 connect Nord, Mitte, Südbahnhof, and Meidling every few minutes. Hourly S15 trains connect Nord, Mitte, Süd, Meidling, and Westbahnhof. S45 trains run every 15 minutes between Hütteldorf and Heiligenstadt.

Urban transit

You could easily spend a day or two investigating the transit system. Transit passes are available: The 24-hour pass costs 50 schillings; the 72-hour pass, 130 schillings; single fare, 17 schillings. The passes are valid in the innermost region of the Wien area on streetcars, subways, suburban trains, and buses.

This is a route J streetcar — a two-section articulated towing a trailer — and that is most definitely a church beyond it, but it is not San Francisco's J-Church line. The scene is Josefstädter Straße, in front of the U6 Stadtbahn (elevated) station on June 10, 1995.

All the transportation lines are detailed on the VOR map (Verkehrsverbund Ost-Region), well worth the 15 schillings it costs at the information office in the Westbahnhof subway station (and probably lots of other places).

Streetcar lines 6, 18, 62, and 65 and the WLB run through a subway west of Südbahnhof. In the subway are two junction stations — Matzleinsdorfer Platz is the more interesting of the two.

Interurban line

The Wiener Lokalbahn runs between Wien Oper (Karlsplatz) and Baden, 30 kilometers out on the Südbahn. Service is run with streetcars (or so they looked to me one evening) every 15 minutes (table A51a). The passes mentioned above won't get you out as far as Baden — you'll have to buy that on the train. The ride is more suburban than interurban. Should you want to take the fast route back, the ÖBB station at Baden isn't far away. Local trains at 06 past each hour take 57 minutes to Südbahnhof; semi-fast trains at 22 and 56 past take about half that.

Hospital railroad

In the western section of Wien, southwest of the Schonbrunn palace, the Altersheim Lainz, a home for the elderly, has a 500mm gauge railway that moves food and laundry between the buildings using battery and diesel locomotives and hand-braked cars. The best time to visit is late morning, when food and laundry are being moved; there is also a period of activity about 1300. The central kitchen has a yard where airline-type food containers are placed on cars; ditto for the main laundry. The system has about 4 kilometers of track.

Take streetcar 62 from Meidling to Krankenhaus Lainz, two stops from the end of the line. Ed Immel, who told me about this, suggests using the back gate, farther along the streetcar line, rather than the main gate.

Rail museums

If you look out the south side of your train just west of the Westbahnhof, you'll see half a dozen steam locomotives sitting in the open, as if the roundhouse had just been lifted off.

They're part of the Austrian Railway Museum, which is a section of the Technical Museum, located at 212 Mariahilferstraße, about halfway between Westbahnhof and Penzing. The Penzinger Straße stop on streetcar routes 10, 52, and 58 is just west of the museum.

The Wiener Straßenbahnmuseum (Vienna Street Railway Museum) is in the Erdberg carbarn at 109 Erdbergstraße, northeast of the Südbahnhof and southeast of the Mitte Bahnhof. You can take subway line U3 or streetcar lines 18 and 72 to reach the museum. It is open Saturdays, Sundays, and holidays from the beginning of May to the beginning of October, 0900-1600. For information on the museum, telephone 43-1-7909-44900; fax 43-1-7909-44909. During the season the museum is open, streetcars from the museum make a trip around the city, departing from the Otto Wagner Pavilion at Karlsplatz at 1130 and 1330 Saturdays and at 0930, 1130, and 1330 Sundays and holidays. For information on the sightseeing circle tour and tickets inquire at the information office in the Karlsplatz subway station.

Recommended trips
Gmünd and the Waldviertelbahn
Krems an der Donau and the Wachau
Mariazellerbahn
Semmering Pass
East of Wien
Westbahn
Airport

GMÜND AND THE WALDVIERTELBAHN

ÖBB operates steam on the 760mm gauge, 43-kilometer Waldviertelbahn from Gmünd, on the Czech border northwest of Wien, to Groß Gerungs. *Fahrpläne* shows one steam-powered round trip with these caveats: runs on demand, steam power not guaranteed, and special ticket required. The *Thomas Cook European Timetable* says that steam usually runs weekends in October and May and also on holidays and that the extra fare is 40 schillings.

If you want to stay in Gmünd, Karl Zöchmeister recommends the Hotel Konsul, about halfway between the Gmünd station and the Czech border. *Hotels in Austria* lists the Hotel Goldener Stern (****), Stadtplatz 15, A-3950 Gmünd; telephone 43-2852-54545, fax 43-2852-54548. Double with bath, 1080-1380 schillings; single with bath, 620-770 schillings.

Wien FJB	leave	0705		1105	(A8,
Gmünd	arrive	0920		1320	C990)
	Steam		**Regular trains**		
Gmünd	leave	0950	0926	a1335	(A84,
Groß Gerungs	arrive	1150	1045	1454	C991)
Groß Gerungs	leave	1330	1115	a1500	
Weitra	arrive	1459	1207	1552	
Weitra	leave	1650	1208	1604	
Gmünd	arrive	1724	1234	1630	
Gmünd	leave	§1736	1840	1240	1640
Wien FJB	arrive	1938	2055	1455	1855

§ — Sundays

a — Monday through Friday, also Sundays through September

KREMS AN DER DONAU AND THE WACHAU

You can easily cover the line along the north bank of the Donau (Danube) from Krems to St. Valentin in a day. See page 72 in the section on St. Pölten.

MARIAZELLERBAHN

The 760mm gauge electrified Mariazellerbahn is an easy day excursion from Wien. For a description of the route and the schedules, see page 74 in the section on St. Pölten.

SEMMERING PASS

The Südbahn, South Railway, over Semmering Pass is considered the first mountain railway in the world, or at least in Europe. It postdates a few early American lines that did some mountain-climbing — the Pennsylvania line from Philadelphia to Pittsburgh and the Baltimore & Ohio through West Virginia. I confess I was skeptical before I rode it, but I was impressed.

In 1841 the first portion of the line was opened, from Wien to Wiener Neustadt, and a year later the line extended to Gloggnitz, at the base of Semmering Pass. Among the proposals for the mountain route were inclined planes (working like San Francisco cable cars) and horse power. Engineer Karl von Ghega, however, planned an ordinary adhesion line. The mountain portion of the line was opened in 1854, and by 1857 it was possible to travel by train from Wien through Graz to Trieste. The line line loops back and forth, and there are plenty of tunnels and viaducts. The grade is 2.5 percent.

The line was electrified in 1959 and somewhat rebuilt at that time. It has been used for years as a test track for new locomotives — including the diesel-hydraulics built by Krauss-Maffei for Southern Pacific in 1961.

Express trains run hourly over the line. They all stop at Mürzzuschlag, 13 kilometers west of the summit tunnel, at the base of the west ramp. All-stop locals run over the pass every hour or two — see table A5 (table C980 covers the fast trains but not the locals). Pick a sunny day, ride south and note good locations, then work back on local trains, or simply take a local south from Wiener Neustadt and keep your eye open for good spots.

A walking train leads from Semmering to the next station north, Wolfsbergkogel (1.5 kilometers), then to Breitenstein (9.5 kilometers or 6 miles), Klamm (15.5 kilometers), and eventually to Payerbach-Reichenau and Gloggnitz (Boy Scout hiking merit badge distances.)

Payerbach-Reichenau, where the line makes a horseshoe

96   The Railfan Guide to Austria

The EuroCity train Bartok Béla, which runs from Stuttgart, Germany, to Budapest, Hungary, speeds through Parndorf Ort in the flat country about 30 miles southeast of Wien. The class 1014 electric locomotive is one of the newest on the roster of Austrian Federal Railways. It can draw power from both Austria's 15,000-volt catenary and Hungary's 25,000-volt system, and does so as it runs straight through from Vienna to Budapest. Its design earned it a Brunel Award. Photo by Klaus Matzka.

curve, is a good base for walking along the line. About two blocks from the station at the corner of Bahnhofstraße and Hauptstraße is the hotel Payerbacher Hof (Hauptstraße 2, A-2650 Payerbach; phone 43-2666-2430). At the west end of the town, practically in the shadow of the Schwarzaviaduct, is the hotel Österreichischer Hof (Hauptstraße 40, A-2650 Payerbach; phone 43-2666-2697). Neither is listed in *Hotels in Austria*. A steam locomotive is on display at the station, and a few years ago a railway museum was getting under way there.

On the west side of the pass, Zöchmeister advises that accommodations should be easy to find in Mürzzuschlag. Farther along, consider the Hotel Schwarzen Adler in Bruck an der Mur (see page 55).

The Györ-Sopron-Ebenfurt recently acquired diesel cars from the Jenbach works of the same type as the ÖBB 5047 and 5147 cars. A pair is shown here running from Pamhagen toward Neusiedl am See. Photo by Klaus Matzka.

EAST OF WIEN

Counting the way the map folds, eight-ninths of Austria's width is west of Wien and one-ninth to the east. Wien lies at the eastern tip of the Alps, and east of Wien is the Hungarian plain. If your jet lands toward the west at Wien, it will circle to the east over that area — and it won't look like anything you've seen on the travel posters.

There are railroads in that area, too: the main line east to Budapest (tables A7 and C1200), the Pottendorfer line from Wien Meidling to Wiener Neustadt via Pottendorf and lying to the east of the Südbahn, and even a private railway, the Györ-Sopron-Ebenfurt Railway (Raab-Oedenburg-Ebenfurter-Eisenbahn in German), which runs from Ebenfurth to Györ, Hungary, and from Neusiedl am See to Fertöszentmiklös. The Eurailpass is valid on both that railway and MAV, the Hungarian national railroad system. If you have a day free and a Eurailpass in your pocket, consider a day trip to Budapest (it's about 3 hours from Wien) or go to Györ and return on the GSE. A passport is necessary, of course, but not a visa.

WESTBAHN

The Westbahn, the main line from Wien to Salzburg, is likely to be on your itinerary for convenience at the very least. It is one of the principal east-west routes of Europe. It carries hourly trains to Salzburg, other long-distance expresses, local trains at least every couple of hours over all segments of the route, frequent suburban trains as far west as St. Pölten (60 kilometers from Wien), and freight trains.

The line was opened in 1858 from Wien to Linz as the Royal Imperial Empress Elisabeth Railway after a bit more than two years' construction time (that would still be considered fast work today). Electrification began from the west end in 1937, reaching Linz in 1949 and Wien in 1952 (a war intervened).

The initial portion of the Westbahn climbs through the Vienna Woods, which are the eastern tail of the Alps. The line curves and winds, and the many suburban stations should provide photo opportunities.

AIRPORT

This is a necessary trip, unless you've acquired a residency permit. Buses run hourly (half-hourly from late March to early October) between Westbahnhof, Südbahnhof, and Flughafen Wien Schwechat (Vienna Airport). Buses run every 20 minutes between the City Air Terminal in the Hilton near the Mitte station and the airport. See table C989.

S7 suburban trains run half-hourly between Nord, Mitte, and the airport. The trains are made up of older suburban equipment with steep steps and little space for luggage, and they take longer than the buses. The underground station at the airport is utilitarian, but it protects you from the weather and its escalators get you up into the terminal. See tables A92 and C989.

ODDS AND ENDS

THIS SECTION CONTAINS items that are too short to merit sections of their own.

Linz

Linz has a small 900mm gauge streetcar system with just two lines: Line 3, which runs from the Hauptbahnhof, and Line 1, which is a surprising 14 kilometers long. At the end of Line 3 is the meter-gauge Postlingbergbahn, which has the steepest adhesion grade in Europe, 10.5 percent.

Special trains, other museums, steam, etc.

Karl Zöchmeister, head of an ÖBB passenger service department and experienced in organizing and operating excursion and charter trains, graciously offers his assistance to North American railfans planning to visit Austria. He can provide current information on rail events such as steam specials, gourmet trains, and exhibitions. Write to him at:

Gauermanngasse 2-4, A-1010 Wien.
Fax, 43-1-480 1488; e-mail, karl.zoechmeister@pv.oebb.at

A booklet titled *Erlebnis Bahn und Schiff* listing steam excursions and other special trains is available from Austrian National Tourist Offices and from Bahn Total Service, Westbahnhof, A-1150 Wien.

The First Austrian Street Railway and Railway Club (Erste Österreichische Straßenbahn- und Eisenbahn-Klub) has a museum at Straßhof, 23 kilometers and 29 minutes out of Wien Nord on the line to Gänserndorf (tables A9 and A93). It is open Sundays and holidays April through September from 1000 to 1600. The museum has a large collection of steam locomotives. Admission is 50 schillings. For further information, write to the club at Postfach 62, A-1103 Wien.

A friend recommends a visit to the Eisenbahnmuseum Groß Schwechat, operated by the Verband der Eisenbahnfreunde (Association of Railfans). It is located at Groß Schwechat, 15 kilometers from Wien Nord on the S7 suburban line—table 92 (next stop after Groß Schwechat is the airport, Flughafen Wien-Schwechat).

The museum has standard gauge and 600mm gauge track and operates steam locomotives. It is open one weekend a month from April through October, except August, and there is usually someone on the premises late afternoons and most weekends. For current information, write to the Verband der Eisenbahnfreunde, Postfach 28, A-1203 Wien.

Nostalgiebahnen in Kärnten operates the Rosental Dampfbummelzug (Rosental steam local train) Saturday afternoons from late June to early September from Weizelsdorf to Ferlach, where there is a transportation museum. Weizelsdorf is 12 kilometers and 16 minutes from Klagenfurt on the line to Rosenbach (table A66) mentioned in the section on Villach. The schedules are arranged for good connections with ÖBB at Weizelsdorf. For information, write to Nostalgiebahnen in Kärnten, Postfach 27, A-9028 Klagenfurt.

There is an industrial-railway museum at Freiland, 31 kilometers and 50 minutes south of St. Pölten on the local line found in table A11a. The museum is open Sundays from 1000 to 1600, mid-April to early October. The 1994 schedule shows operations on one Sunday each in May, August, and September. For information on dates of operation, write to Feld- und Industriebahnmuseum, A-3183 Freiland.

About an hour east of Villach, half an hour east of Klagenfurt on the main line to Wien (table A6), is the station of Treibach-Althofen. From there the Gurkthalbahn parallels ÖBB north a few kilometers to Pöckstein-Zwischenwässern. The line is narrow gauge and steam; it operates Saturdays, Sundays, and holidays from mid-June to mid-September (departures from Treibach at 1115, 1345, 1515, and 1645). Round-trip fare is 60 schillings. For further information, write to the Gurkthalbahn, Postfach 181, A9010 Klagenfurt.

One station north of Bruck an der Mur is Kapfenberg, southern terminal of the narrow gauge Thörlerbahn, which runs 20 kilometers up the valley of the Thörlerbach to Seebach-Turnau. It operates two or three weekends a month from May through September. Round-trip fare is 120 schillings. Write to Eisenbahnverein Thörlerbahn, Postfach 2, A-8600 Bruck/Mur.

Two stops and 10 minutes west of Attnang-Puchheim and a bit over an hour east of Salzburg on the Westbahn (tables A1 and

C950) is Timelkam, starting point for trains of the Museumsbahn Ampflwang-Timelkam. It operates Saturdays and Sundays in July and August. The 1040 and 1445 departures from Timelkam (1997 schedules) are timed to connect with ÖBB trains. The ride to Ampflwang takes 45 to 50 minutes. At Ampflwang are a locomotive display and a number of good restaurants. For information, write to ÖGEG, the Österreichesches Gesellschaft für Eisenbahngeschichte GmbH (Austrian Society for Railroad History Inc.), Postfach 11, A-4018 Linz, or fax them at 43-732-783657 Monday through Friday mornings.

Discovery

I can't tell you everything about railroads in Austria, and if I did, I would take away the joy of discovery. You have my best wishes for a good trip and for your own pleasure in seeing new things. Tell me about the good stuff I haven't seen.

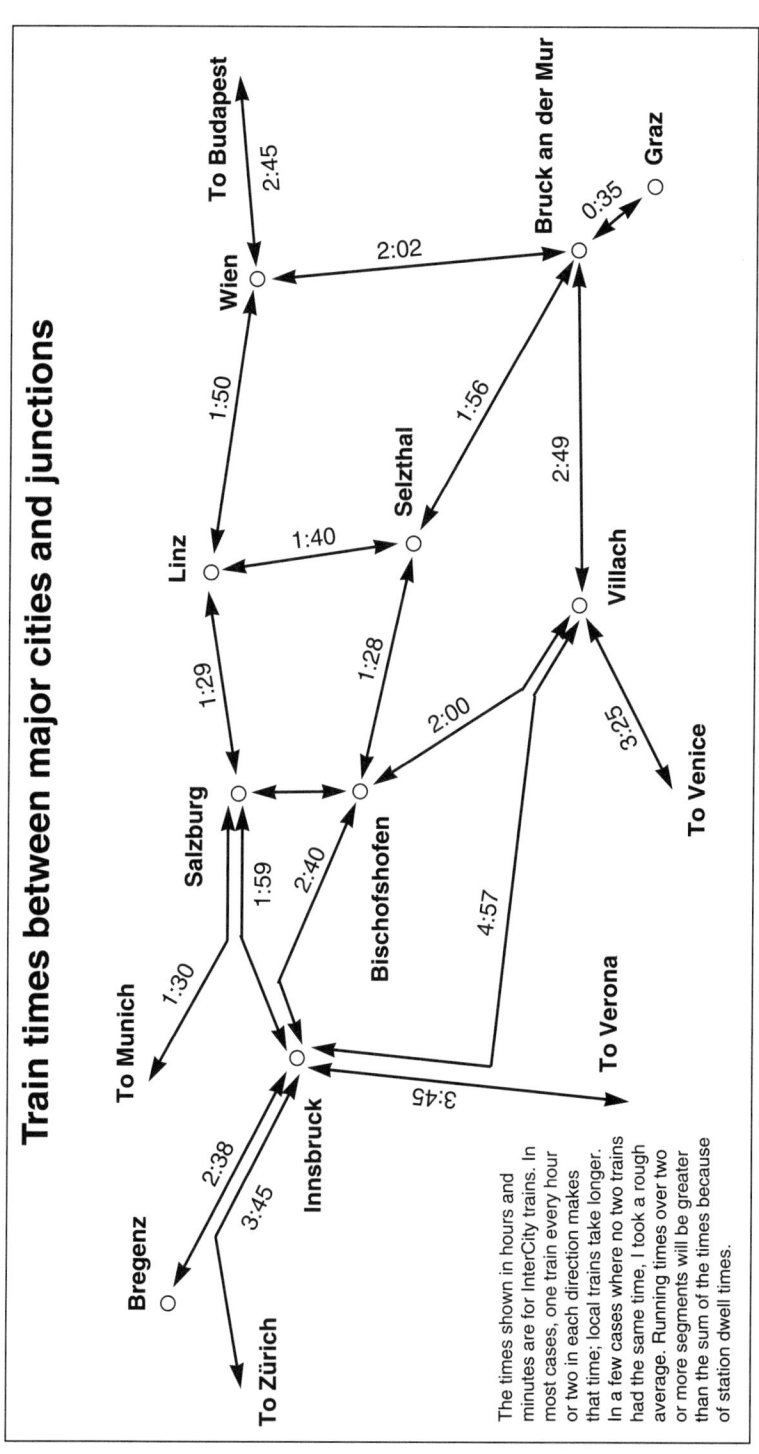

RAILWAY MAP OF AUSTRIA

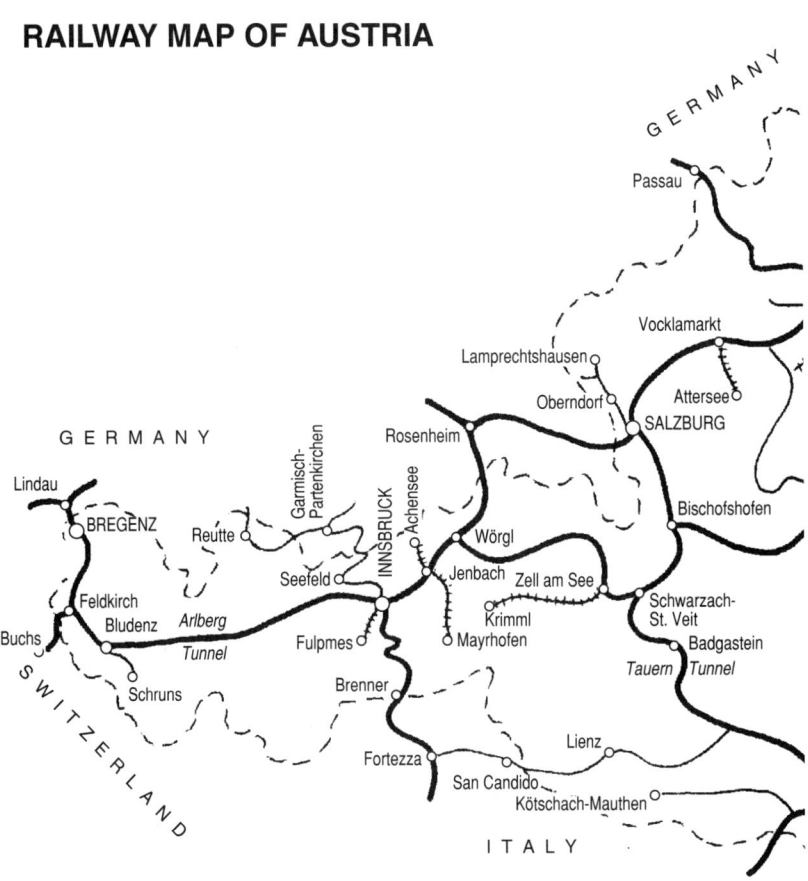

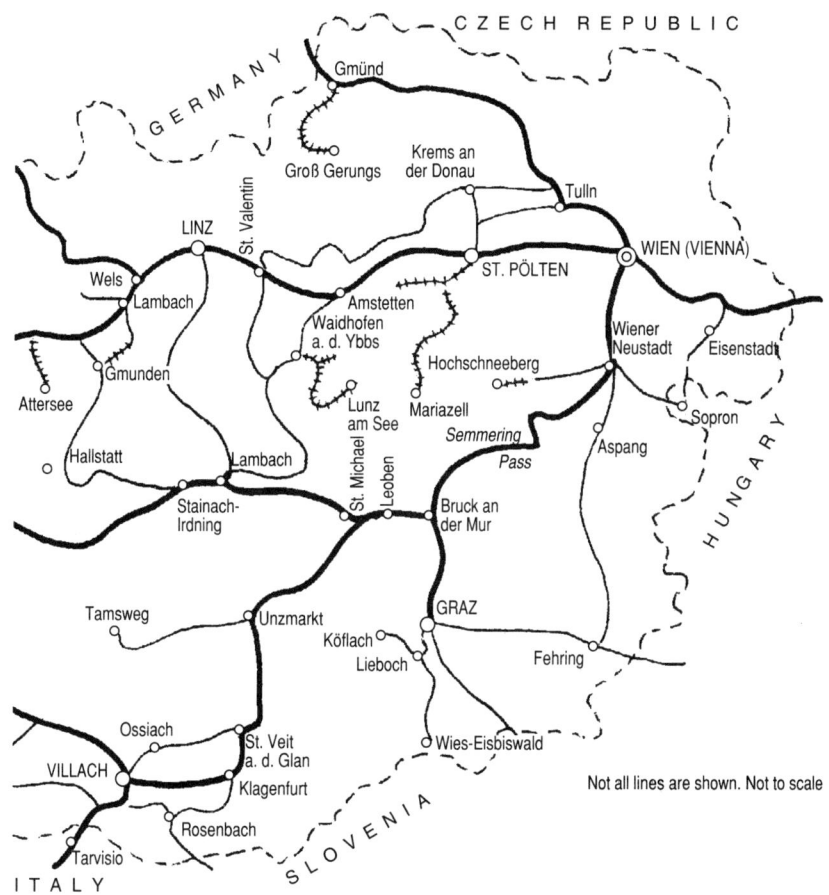

Railway map of Austria   105

INDEX

For subjects that appear in several places, a **boldface** page number indicates the principal entry.

A
Abbeys, 72, 73
Achenseebahn, 68
Air travel, 30
Airlines, 21
Alps, 11
Altersheim Lainz, 94
Amstetten, 44
Architecture of Austria, 13
Arlberg route, 65
Aspangbahn, 63
Attersee, 84
Austrian Federal Railways Locomotives and Multiple Units, 38
Austrian National Tourist Offices, 23, 100
Austrian Open-Air Museum, 62
Austrian Railpass, 25
Austrian Railway Museum, 94

B
Badgastein, 52
Bärnbach, 62
Bischofshofen, 50
Bludenz, 21
Boats, 68, 76, 78, 83, 85
Böckstein, 52
Bregenz, 11, 21
Brenner Pass, Brenner route, 65, 68
Bruck an der Mur, 55
Budapest, Hungary, 98
Burg Hochosterwitz, 89
Burgenland, 12

C
Carinthia, see Kärnten
Checking baggage, 28, 30, 64, 88
Clock, 24-hour, 7
Clothing, 28
Coffee, 33
Cold, catching a, 30
Credit cards, 27
Customs, 27

D
Danube, see Rivers, Donau
Diesel locomotives, 40
Dining car prices, 43
Distances, 6

E
Eating on trains, 43
Eisenbahnmuseum Groß Schwechat, 100
Eisenerz, 47, 56
Eisenstadt, 12
Electric locomotives, 39
Electricity, 32
Enns valley, 47
Erlebnis Bahn und Schiff, 100
Erste Österreichische Straßenbahn- und Eisenbahn-Klub, 100
Erzbergbahn, 47, 56
Eurailpasses, 24, 26
EuroPass, 24
European East Pass, 25

F
Fahrpläne, 2, 7, 26, 37
Feld- und Industriebahnmuseum, 101
Film, 34
Freud, Sigmund, 13
Fulpmes, 69
Furth-Göttweig abbey, 72

G
Gailtalbahn, 87
Geography of Austria, 11
Glossaries
    Basic courtesies, 14
    Hotel terms, 20
    Menu, 16
    Railroad, 14
    Timetable, 19
Gmünd, 95
Gmunden, 80, 83
Gmunden-Vorchdorf Railway, 80
Graz, 12, 60
Graz-Köflacher Bahn, 57, 63
Group tours, 22
Groß Gerungs, 95

Guidebooks, 23
Gurkthalbahn, 101
Györ-Sopron-Edenfurt Railway, 98

H
Haag am Hausruck, 81
Hallstatt, 82
Heurigers, 72, 90
Hieflau, 47
History of Austria, 9
Hochosterwitz, 89
Hofburg, 90
Holidays, 23
Holy Roman Empire, 9
Hospital railroad, 94
Hotel reservation letters, 20
Hotels in Austria, 2, 32
Hotels, about, 32
Hotels, Alte Post, 50
   An der Wien, 90
   Austrotel, 90
   Bayrischer Hof, 79
   City, 86
   Cristall, 90
   Daniel, 61
   Drei Raben, 61
   Europa (Graz), 61
   Europa (Salzburg), 79
   Goldener Stern, 95
   Graf, 72
   Gürtler, 44
   Konsul, 95
   Metropol, 72
   Mosser, 86
   Nordbahn, 90
   Österreichischer Hof, 97
   Payerbacher Hof, 96
   Raffelsbergerhof, 73
   Reichshof, 90
   Sailer, 66
   Schützenhof, 50
   Schwarzer Adler, 55
   Stasta, 90
   Stiegelbräu K&K, 79
   Toleranz, 66
   Wiesler, 60
   Zum Hirschen, 79
   Zur Linde, 45

Hundertwasser, Friedensreich, 13, 62
Hungerberg Bahn, 67

I
Igls, 67
Innsbruck Verkehrsbetriebe, 66
Innsbruck, 21, 65
Intercity train times, 103
International Railway Traveler, 22
Interurban, 94

J
Jenbach, 66, 71
Jet lag, 31

K
Karawanken Tunnel, 87
Kärnten (Carinthia), 12
Kilometers and miles, 6
Klagenfurt, 12, 86
Krems an der Donau, 72
Krimml, 53, 71
Krumpe, 75

L
Lambach-Haag Railway, 81
Lambach–Vorchdorf-Eggenberg Railway, 81
Lands (provinces) of Austria, 11
Language, 14
Laundry, laundromats, 29
Lienz, 70
Linz, 12, 100
Lippizaner horses, 62
Literature of Austria, 13
Lokalbahn Gmunden-Vorchdorf, 80
Lokalbahn Lambach-Haag, 81
Lokalbahn Lambach–Vorchdorf-Eggenberg, 81
Lokalbahn Vöcklamarkt-Attersee, 84
Lokalbahnmuseum (Innsbruck), 67
Lower Austria, 11, 12
Luggage, 27

M
Mallnitz-Obervellach, 52
Maps, 26
Mariazellerbahn, 48, 74
Mayrhofen, 71
Meal prices, 33
Melk abbey, 73, 76
Melk, 76
Miles and kilometers, 6
Mittersill, 53
Model railroad shop, 67
Money, 27
Mozart, 78
Munich, Germany, 21
Murau, 57
Murtalbahn, 57, 64, 88
Museums (rail), 49, 62, 67, 75, 94, 100
Museumsbahn Ampflwang-Timelkam, 101
Museumstramway Mariazell-Erlaufsee, 75
Music of Austria, 12

N
Narrow gauge, 52, 74, 80, 88, 94, 100, 101
Nieder-Österreich, 11, 12
Nostalgiebahn in Kärnten, 101
Notation, 6

O
Ober Grafendorf, 75
Ober-Österreich, 11
Oberndorf, 81
Ossiach, 89
Oststeirer (train), 63
Ötscherland (train), 75

P
Pajamas, 32
Passport, 27
Payerbach-Reichenau, 96
Photographic film, 34
Pinzgauer Lokalbahn, 52
Planning your trip, 21
Post office hours, prices, 34
Postlingbergbahn, 100
Pottendorfer line, 98

Prices, dining car meals, 43
Pronunciation, 16
Provinces (Lands) of Austria, 11
Pustertal (train), 70, 87

R
Raab-Oedenburg-Ebenfurter-Eisenbahn, 98
Rail passes, 24
Railroad initials 42
Railways of Austria, 35
   Locomotive classification, 38
   Locomotives, 38
   Passenger cars, 41
   Principal routes, 36
   Route names, 35
Reservations, hotel, 20
Reservations, seat, trains, 42
Restaurants, meal prices, 33
Riding the trains, 42
Rivers
   Donau (Danube), 11, 44, 47, 72, 76
   Drau, 12
   Enns, 11, 44, 45
   Glan, 89
   Inn, 11
   Laming, 55
   Mur, 55, 57, 60
   Mürz, 55
   Salzach, 11, 50, 53, 78
   Schwarzach, 52
   Ybbs, 44, 49
Rosenbach, 87
Rosentalbahn, 87
Ruprechtshofen, 75

S
St. Pölten, 12, 72
St. Stephan's Cathedral, 90
St. Valentin, 45
St. Veit an der Glan, 89
Salzburg, 11, 21, 78
Salzburger Lokalbahn, 78, 81
Salzkammergut, 51, 78, 82
Salzkammergut Lokalbahn, 84
Schafbergbahn, 83
Schönbrunn Palace, 90
Seat reservations, 42

Seefeld in Tirol, 69
Selzthal, 48, 82
Semmering Pass, 4, 59, 96
Silent Night, 82
Soap, 32
Sound of Music, 78
Souvenirs, 32
Spanish Riding School, 62, 90
Steam, 52, 58, 68, 71, 95, 100, 101
Steam locomotives, 38
Steiermerkische Landesbahnen, 57, 64, 88
Steiermark, 12
Stern & Hafferl, 78, 81, 84
Stern & Hafferl, Umweltkarte (pass), 25
Store hours, 34
Streetcars, 41, 61, 66, 80, 93, 100
Stubaitalbahn, 69
Styria (Steiermark), 12

T
Tamsweg, 58
Tauern Tunnel, 52
Telephone numbers, 32, 90
Thomas Cook European Timetable, 2, 7, 26, 37
Thörlerbahn, 101
Timetables, 2, 7, 26, 37
Tipping, 33
Tirol (Tyrol), 11
Tourist offices, 23
Train times between cities, 103
Trains Magazine, 6, 22
Tramway-Museum Graz, 62
Tramways and Light Railways of Austria, Hungary, and Yugoslavia, 41

Transit passes, 25
Travelers checks, 27
Trip planning, 21
Tyrol, see Tirol

U
Umweltkarte (Stern & Hafferl), 25, 84
Unzmarkt, 57
Upper Austria, 11

V
Val Pusteria (train), 70, 87
Vienna, see Wien, 90
Villach, 70, 86
Vöcklamarkt-Attersee, 84
Von Ghega, Karl, 96
Von Ryan's Express, 69
Vorarlberg, 11

W
Wachau, 73
Waidhofen an der Ybbs, 48
Waldviertelbahn, 95
Waterfall, Krimml, 53
Weather, 22, 78
Weißenkirchen, 73
Wien, 12, 46, 77, 90
  airport, 99
  stations, 91
  transit, 92
Wiener Lokalbahn, 94
Ybbstalbahn, 48

Z
Zell am See, 53
Zillertalbahn, 53, 71
Zürich, Switzerland, 21

Notes

Notes

Other guidebooks in this series are:

The Railfan Guide to Switzerland	$17.95
The Reluctant Railfan's Introduction to Europe	$17.95

Available where you bought this book, or order direct from:

George H. Drury
4139 West McKinley Court
Milwaukee, Wisconsin 53208-2765
Phone and fax: 414-344-7747
E-mail: GeorgDrury@aol.com

Shipping: $3.05 for the first book ordered; $1.05 for each additional book ordered at the same time.

Wisconsin residents please add applicable sales tax.

Books in preparation:

The Railfan Guide to Germany
The Railfan Guide to Britain and Ireland

Watch for advertisements in *Trains* and *International Railway Traveler*